IVAN MOSCOVICH

Deviously Difficult

Mind-Bending Puzzles

Sterling Publishing Co., Inc.
New York

Deviously Difficult Mind-Bending Puzzles
Was commissioned, edited, designed, and produced by
Imagine Puzzles Ltd.,
20 Lochaline Street
London W6 9SH
United Kingdom

Managing director: **Hal Robinson**
Consultant editor: **David Bodycombe**
Editor: **Alison Moore**
Project manager: **Tamiko Rex**
Art editor: **Beatriz Waller**
Copy editor: **Ruth Binney**

Library of Congress Cataloging-in-Publication Data Available

2   4   6   8   10   9   7   5   3

Published by Sterling Publishing Co., Inc.
387 Park Avenue South, New York, NY 10016
by arrangement with Imagine Puzzles Ltd, London
Artwork and text © 2004 by Imagine Puzzles Ltd.
Distributed in Canada by Sterling Publishing
c/o Canadian Manda Group, 165 Dufferin Street
Toronto, Ontario, Canada M6K 3H6
Distributed in Great Britain by Chrysalis Books Group PLC
The Chrysalis Building, Bramley Road, London W10 6SP, England
Distributed in Australia by Capricorn Link (Australia) Pty. Ltd.
P.O. Box 704, Windsor, NSW 2756, Australia

Sterling ISBN 1-4027-1810-1

CONTENTS

PREFACE

I have been designing and inventing puzzles, games, and toys for the past 30 years or so. During that period I also conceived and created a science museum with, among other things, a planetarium. Today I devote all my time to the creation of games and toys—and enjoy every moment of it.

Many of the games and puzzles in this book are completely original; others are novel adaptations of more traditional games. My hope is that this book will convey my enthusiasm for and fascination with games and my approach to their creation and design. It combines entertainment with an intellectual challenge, through which a great number of concepts basic to art, science, and mathematics may be tackled.

This is an open-ended book; there are many opportunities for readers to modify games in their own way, and to invent new variations. I hope that this will cause a chain reaction: You will play the games, try to solve the problems, and be stimulated to create your own rules and designs, your own games, puzzles, and esthetically pleasing structures.

Despite the diversity of topics included here, there is an underlying continuity in these puzzles: an interplay between geometry and combinatorics (the different ways in which objects can be arranged). All the games and puzzles are designed so that they can easily be made and solved by the average enthusiast. They do not require special skills or materials, most require only cardboard and paint. Some puzzles are best solved through trial and error, so the **Cut-outs** section on pages 99–127 has pieces you can use for some of the puzzles. Color is important, and the many colored illustrations depict examples not just of games, but of the beautiful designs and patterns that arise out of them.

These are not just numerically inspired visual patterns. They can excite the mind and suggest new ideas and insights, new modes of thought, and creative expression. In fact, the creation of such compositions may become for you an exciting activity in its own right.

The topics I have selected are biased toward visual geometrical concepts, with a strong emphasis on structure and pattern, rather than numerical concepts and word games. This bias is, of course, intended. I have always been fascinated by the interaction of geometry and combinatorics, two powerful disciplines that can lead to so many surprising discoveries and complexities, all by taking a small number of basic elements as building blocks and using them according to simple rules.

The book is designed so that each item stands alone (even if it is in fact related to others), so you can dip in at will without the frustration of cross-referencing. I hope you enjoy *Deviously Difficult Mind-Bending Puzzles* as much as I have enjoyed creating it for you.

IVAN MOSCOVICH

PROBLEM SOLVING AND CREATIVITY

Throughout this book you will be using problem-solving skills and will, I hope, learn a little about how your brain functions. Thinking can be hard work; hence the natural human tendency to do as little of it as possible! This is visible in the hit-and-run approach to problem solving: Pick the first solution that comes to mind and run with it. This way, our minds become trapped in their own preconceptions.

In order to skirt around these **conceptual blocks** we need to use **creativity**, which can be thought of as consisting of three parts:

■ **Innovation**—It is impossible to be creative if you merely adapt someone else's work.

■ **Added value**—Creativity must have a practical use at some time. Sometimes this use may not be immediately apparent.

■ **Internal motivation**—This is the will to be curious and to go the extra mile to explore something. In other words, do not just answer a question but go on to set yourself your own questions.

To get your brain in gear, try to stretch your creativity with these warm-up puzzles.

The impossible domino bridge problem

At first sight the structure above is impossible to build. But if you think about it the right way, you can work out how to do it and even build it yourself!

ANSWER page 88

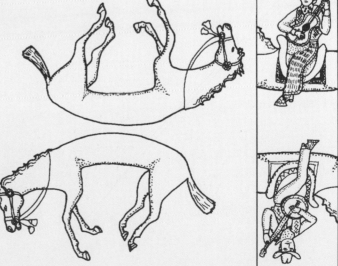

The horse-and-rider problem

Using only your eyes, can you work out how to mount the riders on their horses?

ANSWER page 88

PROBLEM SOLVING AND CREATIVITY

The circles-coloring problem
First, take a look at the figure below. Using the same logic, color the figure underneath it.

ANSWER page 88

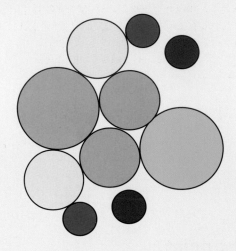

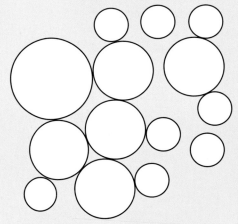

Who was...Samuel Loyd?
He was born in Philadelphia in 1841, and was America's equivalent of Britain's Henry Dudeney. Between them, they created and popularized many puzzles in the late 19th century, including the T-puzzle below. By the age of 17, Loyd was recognized as the foremost American chess problem deviser.
In later life he sold numerous puzzles and games, including a prize version of the infamous 15-square sliding block puzzle that was impossible to complete.

The classic T-puzzle
Copy and cut out the four pieces, and use them to form a perfect capital letter T. Not so easy, is it? This is a classic example of how an apparently easy problem can lead to a conceptual block.

ANSWER page 88

The square game
Here's a creativity exercise to tackle. Draw a square. Done that? OK, now do it at least nine more times. Then take a look in the answers section.

ANSWER page 88

PROBLEM SOLVING AND CREATIVITY

See if you can spot the tricks and twists in these lateral thinking challenges.

From X to Y
Replace X and Y with different letters so that these statements are correct:

$$10X = 50Y$$
$$20X = 68Y$$
$$30X = 86Y$$

ANSWER page 88

Speed demon
Pakistani pace bowler Shoaib Akhtar became the first man to bowl a cricket ball at 100 miles per hour. How can the average person propel something at this speed without using any equipment?

ANSWER page 88

Cheating the heating
In a detached house with central heating, it is possible to make the house **warmer** by turning **down** the temperature control on some radiators. How?

ANSWER page 88

Get the point?
How many arrows can be seen here?

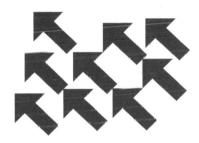

ANSWER page 88

Animal magic
Using each symbol below only once, form the eight-letter name of a mammal.

e h a t
d u l e

ANSWER page 88

Very handy
I need a pair of rubber gloves. I have 50 gloves in a drawer—24 are for the left hand and 26 are for the right hand. If I select gloves at random, what is the least number of rubber gloves that I need to pick in order to have a usable pair?

ANSWER page 88

LINES AND LINKAGES

In this chapter we will look at straight lines, so let's get familiar with them.

The dimensions of space begin with a single point. "A point," said Euclid, "is position without size." Thereafter, the first dimension begins with a line. To build a line, we observe the trace of a moving point whose direction does not alter.

So let's suppose we are engineers with some strong, thin rods. A **linkage** is a system of these rods connected to each other by movable joints, or fixed by pivots about which they can turn freely. Given a number of rigid rods, can a linkage be found that will produce, by the **motion** of one of its points, a straight line?

It is simple to see that pivoting a single rod at one end produces a circular motion. The trick is to construct straight-line motion in the absence of a fixed straight line.

This problem comes from a practical background—the natural motion produced by a steam engine is rotary. While it can be converted to straight-line motion by a piston, this requires bearings that are subject to wear. The first practical solution, devised by **James Watt** (1736–1819), the inventor of the steam engine, was only approximate. The true curve of motion was an elongated figure 8, a segment of which was close enough to a straight line for Watt's purposes (see **C** below).

The first mechanical device to produce exact straight-line motion was **Peaucellier's Linkage**, invented in 1864 (see **D** below). Have a go at making one yourself using strips of cardboard and butterfly-style paperclips.

Before we leave this topic, consider this: If a dot has no dimensions, a line has one dimension, a square has two dimensions, and a cube has three, what comes next? It's called a **hypercube** and can be imagined either as a line of 3-D cubes or a single cube of computer data that changes over time (the fourth dimension).

**HOW TO CREATE
A STRAIGHT LINE**
A By the ancient rope-stretching method—stretching a thread or rope between two points
B By folding a piece of paper
C By using Watt's Linkage
D By using Peaucellier's Linkage

A
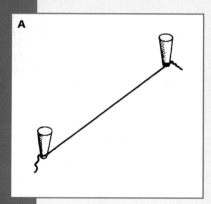

B
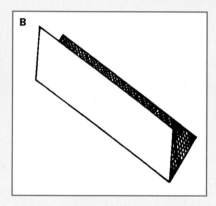

C
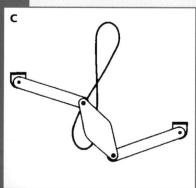

D
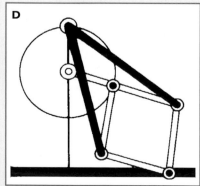

Flexible linkages

On the far right is a representation of a **dodecahedron** (a 12-sided solid) made from 30 flexible links. Note how three links join at any one point. Because the links are flexible, the figure can be moved around to create a remarkable variety of forms: a **cylinder**, a **star**, a ten-sided **polygon** (**decagon**), and an object resembling a flying saucer. Much of the beauty of the original regular shape is retained by these distortions, and the extra lack of regularity and familiarity can arouse our interest. Other geometrical forms can be built from links and subjected to distortions, with equally intriguing results.

Who was...Euclid?

He was a Greek mathematician born around 300 BC. He is well known for his work *Elements*, a comprehensive 13-volume treatise on many aspects of mathematics with an emphasis on geometry.

It is unclear whether he discovered everything contained in the work himself or reorganized the work of other mathematicians.

Nevertheless, modern versions of Euclid's *Elements* are still used in some schools and universities today—more than 2200 years after they were originally written.

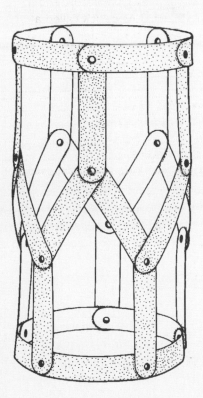

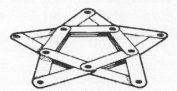

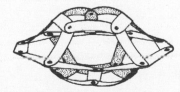

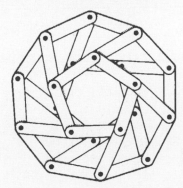

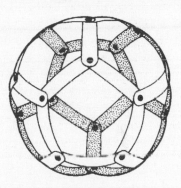

THE DODECAHEDRON

This is one of the regular (Euclidean) solids. The others are the tetrahedron, cube, octahedron, and the icosahedron.

THE GREAT DIVIDE

Farmer Giles was looking to see how best to divide up his square field for the coming season. He can grow a different crop in each fenced-off area. Due to draconian planning regulations, any fences he erects must run in a straight line across the full length of the field. He wondered how many types of crops he would be able to grow and, being an inquisitive countryman with nothing better to do, he decided to find out...

Rural areas

The farmer found that his field divides neatly into two regions using one straight fence. A second fence can divide each of these regions into two again, giving a total of four regions, so he will be able to grow four crops.
Can a third fence divide all four of these parts in two? If so, there would be eight regions formed by three lines. But in fact there are only seven: The third line can be made to pass through three of the previous four regions, but it cannot encounter all of them. As a result, only seven areas can be formed by building three fences.

A Farmer Giles wondered how many regions at most could be formed by four straight fences across the field. What do you think?

B How many different crops could the farmer grow if he had five fences?

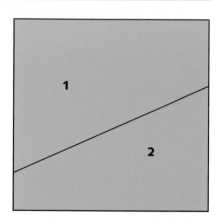

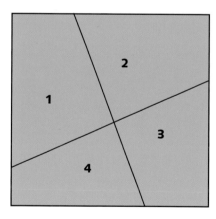

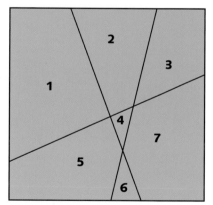

C Can you guess a general rule for the number of regions formed by a given number of fences?
D Finally, can you put your rule into the form of a formula?

ANSWER page 88

THE GREAT DIVIDE

De-fence-less

Farmer Gill, who lived down the lane from Giles, didn't have a square boundary to start with. She has the rather odd-shaped land shown. She used just six straight fences that enclosed eight triangles, some of which overlap. Note that there are three different sizes of triangle—find them in the diagram before continuing. Not wanting to be upstaged, Farmer Giles found a completely different (and simpler) way of erecting six straight fences to enclose eight triangular regions. However, his solution uses only **two** different sizes of triangle. Can you find his method?

HINT A certain flag may help you.

ANSWER page 89

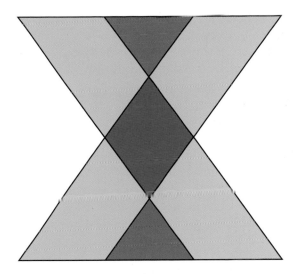

Pizza palaver

How can you cut a circular pizza into eight pieces using three straight cuts of a knife? Each piece must have the same amount of topping and crust.

ANSWER page 89

Cutting the cake

Suppose you had a cake in the shape of a cube. You can cut the cake only three times, but you may rearrange the pieces after each cut if you wish. What is the largest number of pieces into which you can cut the cake? The pieces do not have to be the same size.

ANSWER page 89

LINE MEETS LINE

Jemma, inspired by her glossy interior decoration magazines, got out her brush and paints and was ready to turn the magnolia wall in her living room into a riot of color. The only question was what to draw? And what to do about that drab window?

Weld done

Jemma wanted to put fancy strips of leading onto her square window. The thin strips of lead had to be kept straight, and whenever two strips overlapped she had to weld them together. It stands to reason that any two strips, if not parallel, had to meet in exactly one weld point—the **intersection**. Similarly, three strips of lead required three welds at most and, in the worst case scenario, four strips needed six welds.

Jemma wondered what the general solution was. In other words, what is the largest number of welds required if she used **n** strips, with each strip oriented in a unique direction? Here's a hint: To get the maximum number of welds, each strip has to cross all the others. Can this always be arranged?

ANSWER page 89

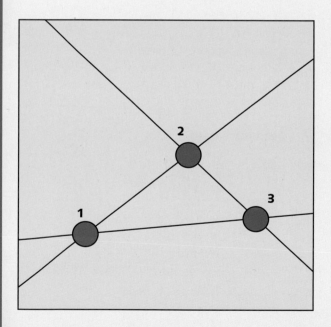

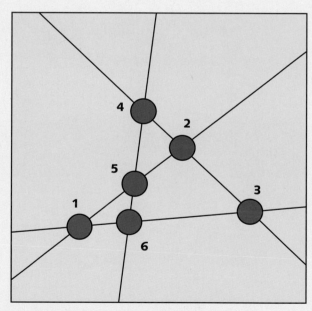

Art Deco-ration

Jemma decided on an Art Deco design to paint onto her wall. She used a ruler and pen to draw just seven straight lines (she didn't want to tire out her creativity too quickly). Wherever a triangle had formed, she painted that area red. As you can see, her chosen design formed six triangles. Could you have done better?

ANSWER page 89

Gone to pot

Jemma had just about finished her room when, to her horror, she realized that her Feng Shui was all awry. Her ten plant pots were all over the place, sending her karma straight out of the window. She found a pleasant arrangement (illustrated) in which the ten plant pots lay on just five different lines. Each line contains four plant pots. Can you find at least one other solution, completely different in appearance from this one, that satisfies the same criteria?

ANSWER page 89

THROUGH THE MIDDLE

MI7 was very happy with its new automated reconnaissance robot, B3RT. The machine was superbly designed for detecting bugs and booby traps in the most demanding conditions. But B3RT couldn't turn very quickly, so his movements were limited to straight lines and a few turns. This worked fine, until one day someone hit on a problem...

Nine areas

MI7 would like B3RT to travel through the nine suspect areas shown. However, time constraints limit B3RT to changing his route only by rotating on the spot on three occasions at most. (This would be equivalent to drawing four straight lines through the dots without lifting your pencil.) B3RT can, however, start and finish wherever he likes.
Can you see the route that B3RT should take?

ANSWER page 89

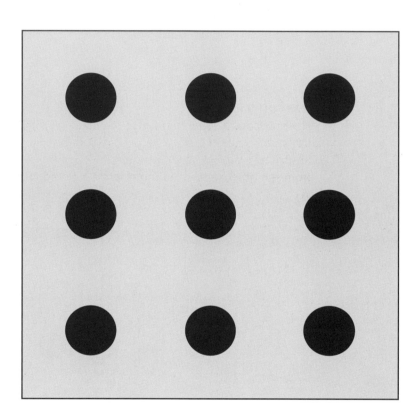

Sneaky solution

Can you see a clever way of solving the **Nine areas** puzzle by changing B3RT's route just twice? In other words, by drawing three continuous straight lines instead of four?

ANSWER page 89

Twelve areas

MI7 was planning big things for B3RT. Suppose he took on a larger mission in which he would have to investigate the 12 areas shown. Starting and finishing at any point, what is the fewest number of continuous straight lines needed to travel through the exact center of every area?

ANSWER page 89

Sixteen areas

Now suppose B3RT has to travel through the center of these 16 areas using six continuous lines. Because MI7 is afraid of losing B3RT in such a large area, they want him to return to wherever he started from—in other words, the route forms a closed loop. Can you find such a solution?

ANSWER page 89

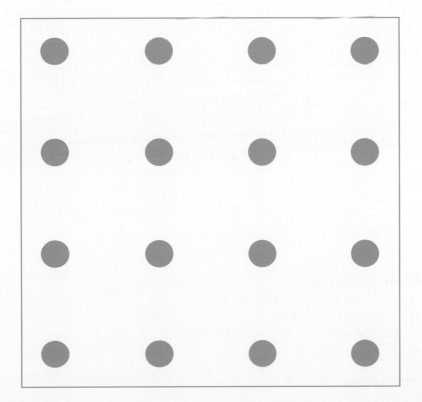

EULER'S PROBLEM

Misha is a schoolboy who lives in the Russian town of Kaliningrad. The town is famous in the field of mathematics because, when it was known as Königsberg, a mathematician named Leonhard Euler was intrigued by its seven bridges. Before going to school one morning, Misha decided to see if he could solve Euler's problem for himself...

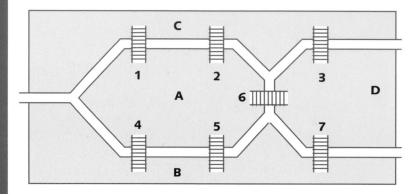

Bridge the gaps

According to the legend in a book Misha borrowed from the library, the people of the town wondered if it was possible to go for a walk, crossing each bridge only once before returning home. Can it be done? The **At a stroke** puzzle opposite may give you insight into how to tackle this.

ANSWER page 90

? What is...topology?

Topology is the branch of mathematics that looks at the fundamental connectedness of objects. For example, the world-famous map of the London Underground bears no relation to the actual routes that the trains take. The tunnels are far more wiggly and the scale is deceptive. However, the map captures the essential nature of how the tracks connect. In the case of the bridges of Königsberg, we can represent the real situation topologically using diagrams such as those illustrated here.

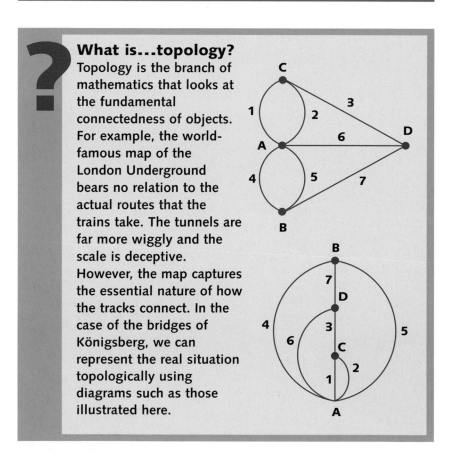

EULER'S PROBLEM

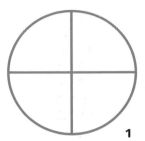

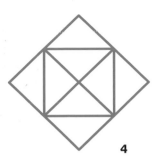

1

2

3

4

At a stroke

Misha's library book tells the story of the Königsberg bridge legend. However, something caught his eye immediately. On the inside cover of the book Misha noticed four differently shaped stamps, presumably used to indicate which librarian lent that particular book. He tried tracing each figure without lifting his pencil from the paper, drawing each line once only. He found that some diagrams were impossible—which ones? Can you give Misha a general rule to help him identify which diagrams can be traversed in this way?

HINT Odd numbers

ANSWER page 90

? Did you know...

Any political map—that is, a map in which no bordering countries share the same color—can be completed using just four colors. In 1976, mathematicians Kenneth Appel and Wolfgang Haken proved that four colors are sufficient no matter how large or complex the map. It was the first major proof that required the use of a computer because there were 1,482 essentially different sub-maps to consider. It took 50 days of computations to arrive at the result.

? Who was...Leonhard Euler?

He was a Swiss mathematician who lived from 1707 to 1783 and wrote up more mathematical research than anyone else in history. He popularized the use of the Greek letter pi (π) to represent the ratio between a circle's circumference and its diameter. He had an excellent memory and so was able to keep working even though he became completely blind in later life. His party trick was said to have been reciting Virgil's entire *Aeneid* from memory.

Not impossible after all

Thinking laterally, how could you actually draw one of the seemingly impossible diagrams from the **At a stroke** puzzle without taking your pencil off the paper?

ANSWER page 90

TWIST AND TURN

TRIANGLES 2

Charlie didn't want to do his math homework. It was geometry tonight...ugh! What use could knowing about "glide reflections" be? He was too busy blasting alien craft from the planet Zaarg to pieces on his game console. Little did he know that, in a tenuous way, he was witnessing his homework in action.

Originally, computers generated graphics by drawing small dots called **pixels** (picture elements) arranged in rows and columns. This technique is called **raster graphics**.

The majority of computer games these days use 3-D graphics to create startlingly realistic worlds and animated characters. Believe it or not, most of these worlds are created using the humble triangle. So whether you're swooning over Lara Croft or admiring Super Mario's mustache, you're actually looking at millions of tiny triangles. Round shapes such as circles are created by drawing lots and lots of thin triangles together. This technique is called **vector graphics**.

To move these triangles around the screen, the computer needs to transform them in three dimensions. Among the possible types of transformations, the important ones are the **rigid motions** or **isometries**, which move figures but do not change their shape or size. (The name is from the Greek: *isos*, the same; and *metros*, measure.)

? Did you know...
The *–gon* ending of the word "polygon" comes from the Greek word *gony*, meaning knee.

There are four basic types of isometry of the plane:

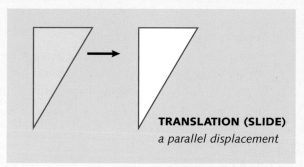

TRANSLATION (SLIDE)
a parallel displacement

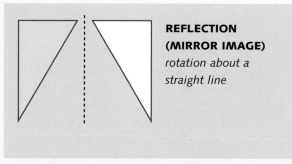

REFLECTION (MIRROR IMAGE)
rotation about a straight line

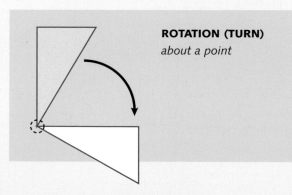

ROTATION (TURN)
about a point

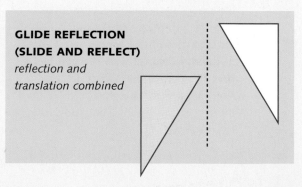

GLIDE REFLECTION (SLIDE AND REFLECT)
reflection and translation combined

Child's play

Little did Charlie know that his baby brother, Angus, had already got the hang of isometries. On his Fancy Games activity set were nine holes through which nine corresponding building blocks could be placed. For instance, Angus noticed that there were two different ways in which the isosceles triangle (shape 2) could be posted through the hole. For the other eight shapes, can you work out how many ways there are of fitting the kiddie blocks into the holes on the right?

HINT They are in a logical order.

ANSWER page 90

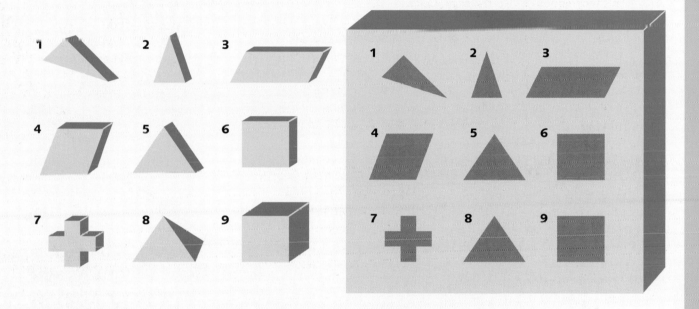

Did you know...

A Playstation 2 can process around 66 million different triangles in three-dimensional space every single second. As well as determining the position, this console can also apply a texture (pattern) and special lighting to each triangle. Even with all these fancy effects enabled, it can still draw up to 20 million triangles per second.

Missing length

Two sides of an isosceles triangle (shape 2 above) are 4 and 9 units long. What is the length of the third side?

ANSWER page 90

A new angle

Contrary to popular belief, the angles of a triangle do not necessarily total 180 degrees. Can you see how it might be possible to draw a triangle that contains three right angles, totaling 270 degrees?

ANSWER page 90

DO NOT EAT BEANS

Most of us have heard of Pythagoras, but his history is somewhat mysterious, as he wrote nothing down. He was a Greek philosopher and mathematician who lived in the 6th century BC. In about 530 BC Pythagoras settled in a Greek colony in Italy where he founded a religious, political, and philosophical movement known as Pythagoreanism. This movement was obsessed with the significance of numbers and shapes, and it began, in essence, a branch of mathematics called **number theory**. However, Pythagoras also had a number of more unusual beliefs and prophecies, including "do not eat beans."

The Egyptian triangle

The principle behind right-angled triangles with whole numbers on every side was known before Pythagoras—he was merely credited with the first proof. For instance, the surveyors of ancient Egypt are said to have used a 3-4-5 triangle to construct near perfect right angles. To see this for yourself, divide a rope into 12 equal parts by making knots or marks. Use it to form a triangle whose sides are 3, 4, and 5 units long. The angle between the 3-unit and 4-unit sides will be a right angle. The 5-unit side is called the **hypotenuse**.

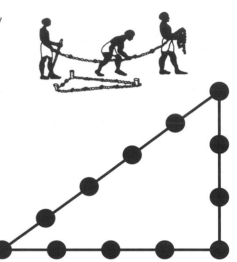

    Note that $3^2 + 4^2 = 9 + 16 = 25 = 5^2$. In fact, as long as $a^2 + b^2 = c^2$, where **a** and **b** are the lengths of the two shorter sides, and **c** is the length of the hypotenuse, the triangle must contain a right angle. Pythagoras' Theorem states that **the square of the hypotenuse is the sum of the squares of the other two sides**. Although the 3-4-5 triangle is the best known, there are infinitely many "Pythagorean Triples." Another example is 5-12-13.

100% proof

Can you see how this diagram helps you prove Pythagoras' Theorem?

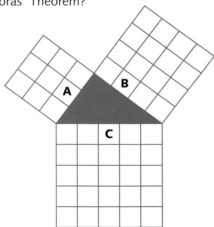

ANSWER page 90

Third base

Two sides of a right-angled triangle are 8 and 17 units long and the length of the third side is a whole number. What is the length of the third side?

ANSWER page 90

Did you know...

Pythagoras' Theorem is officially the most proven theorem in the history of mathematics. In 1940, a book containing over 370 different proofs was published, including contributions from Leonardo da Vinci and James Garfield, the 20th president of the U.S.

DO NOT EAT BEANS

Pythagorean puzzle

Here's a simple jigsaw puzzle you can do by re-creating these six shapes on cardboard or paper (see **cut-out** on page 99).

A First, construct a square on the hypotenuse of the right-angled triangle using the five remaining pieces.
B Now move those pieces and form two squares—one on each of the other sides.

When you have completed both steps, you have not only solved this puzzle but proved the Pythagorean Theorem!

ANSWER page 90

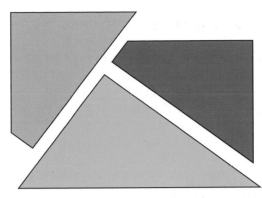

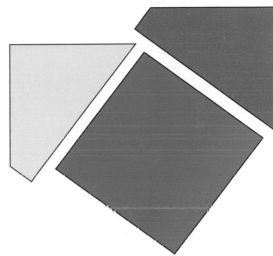

Did you know...

Although infinitely many solutions exist for $a^2 + b^2 = c^2$, no solution exists for $a^3 + b^3 = c^3$. In fact, no solution exists for $a^n + b^n = c^n$, no matter which whole numbers you choose for a, b, and c, for values of n greater than 2—incredible! This is known as **Fermat's Last Theorem**, after the French mathematician Pierre de Fermat.

For over 350 years, many mathematicians offered proofs, but they were all found to have flaws. Cheekily, Fermat himself once wrote, "I have discovered a truly remarkable proof of this which this margin is too small to contain." The eventual full proof by Andrew Wiles, an English mathematician at Princeton University, with the help of Richard Taylor of Cambridge University, was published in May 1995. It is around 130 pages long.

Why is it...called Pythagoras' Theorem, and not Pythagoras' Theory? A **theorem** is something that has been proved. A **theory** is a potential explanation that seems likely but has not yet been proved.

GRAPH-ICAL ANALYSIS

Janice makes jewelry in a beachside resort in Florida. Tourists enjoy rifling through the different knicknacks on display in her small shop on a narrow street near the sea. Her signature pieces involve connecting together clasps with pieces of silver wire and, having made these items for several years, Janice was getting rather adept at calculating the number of essentially different designs she could create...

Five important graph families

Little did Janice know that she was analyzing a branch of mathematics called graph theory. A **graph** describes a system of dots (**vertices** or **nodes**) connected by lines (**edges**). Two graphs are considered the same, or topologically equivalent, if corresponding nodes are joined in corresponding ways. Graphs are an abstract representation of many real-life problems. For example, a novelist might write a book from start to finish, similar to a graph called a **path**. A farmer has an ongoing routine of jobs to do throughout the year, like the **cycle** graph. A toy that has several parts that must be made before the whole toy is assembled is similar to a **star** or, if the assembly requires several stages, a **tree**. And a business meeting might look like a **wheel**—everyone interacts with everyone else. By analyzing a graph, the most efficient ordering of tasks for a particular situation may be deduced.

Deluxe jewelry

Some customers prefer to buy Janice's deluxe jewelry. These pieces have a pleasingly symmetrical design, even though they take longer to make.
The illustrations show how many wires are needed to connect two to six clasps so that there is a wire from every clasp to every other clasp. Can you predict how many wire connections are needed if Janice continues the series with seven, eight, or more clasps?

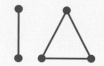

ANSWER page 90

Runes

Janice makes beautiful runes that have a line design drawn on them. The designs are created by joining every clasp on the perimeter with two other clasps to form one continuous loop. The diagrams show that with three clasps only one design is possible. With four clasps, three designs are possible—two of these appear similar but are not identical because they look different when hung from the main clasp. How many designs would be possible with five clasps? Six? What's the general rule?

ANSWER page 90

	Path	Cycle	Star	Tree	Wheel
2					
3					
4					
5					
6					

Galaxy game

This puzzle game is based on an original design by the 19th-century Irish mathematician William Rowan Hamilton.

Setup

You can play this game by writing the numbers in pencil, but it's best if you cut out the 20 disks numbered from 1 to 20 (see **cutout** on page 99).

How to play

The aim is to visit all the planets of the galaxy (the circles) in one continuous trip. Place the **1** counter on any circle you like. This is your home planet. Now fly to any adjoining planet and place the **2** counter there. Continue around the galaxy, placing the disks in strict number order from 1 to 20. The aim of the game is to visit every planet once, but you **must** return to your home planet at the end of the trip!

ANSWER page 90

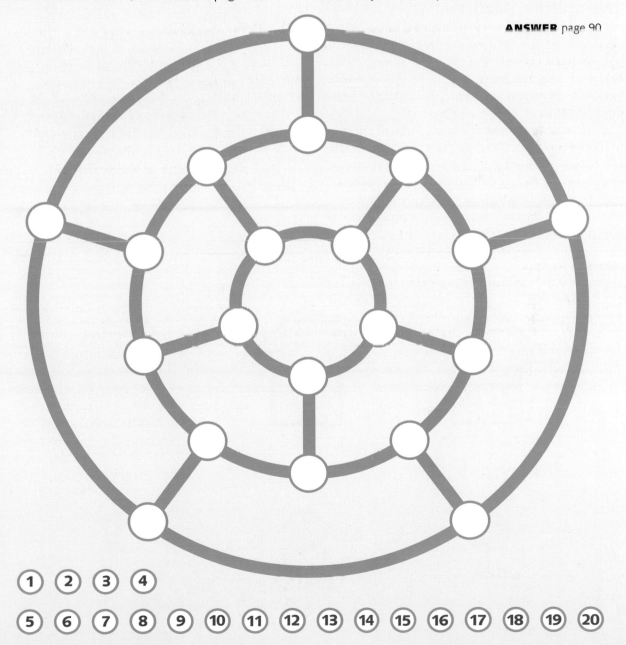

VERY TWO-DIMENSIONAL

There's much cutthroat competition among the utility industries in Smallville. Given that pipelines and wires sometimes have to share the same holes in the ground, sabotage and industrial espionage cannot be eliminated. Here we look at the problems created if each company wishes to stay well away from the others...

The utilities problem

If a network of connections can be drawn on a 2-D plane without any lines crossing (other than at a node or junction), then it is said to be **planar**. For example, the graph formed by the components of an electrical circuit on one side of a printed circuit board must be planar to avoid short circuits.

In this problem, each house in Smallville wants to receive gas, water, and electricity. However, each company is adamant that its pipes and wires cannot cross over any from a rival utility. Can you connect each house with each utility in such a way that no lines intersect (in other words, form a planar graph)? It can be done.

ANSWER page 91

Did you know...

Although our utility graph has only two dimensions, and everyday life has three dimensions, some scientists believe that the universe may have as many as **ten** dimensions? This idea, called the **superstring theory**, is the best candidate for a theory that binds the entire universe together. In this theory, everything in the universe consists of fantastically small strings, which are vibrating and spinning in a ten-dimensional space.

The strings are so small that 100,000,000,000,000,000,000 of them laid end to end would equal the diameter of one proton.

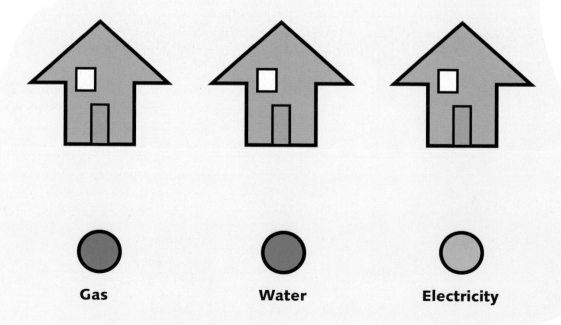

Gas   **Water**   **Electricity**

Sprouts

Here's a clever little game you can play with planar graphs. All you need is a pen, a blank piece of paper…and an opponent.

Setup

Draw two dots on the paper, several inches apart.

Procedure

Players take turns. On your turn connect up any two dots, then draw a new third dot somewhere in the middle of the line. On the first move, there is only one move you can make. However, the situation gets more complex as the game continues.

Rules

A No line may cross any other line (that is, the graph must be planar).

B No node (junction) can have more than three lines connecting to it. You can put a circle around any dot connected by three lines to help you avoid it.

Outcome

The loser is the first player who finds it impossible to make a valid move.

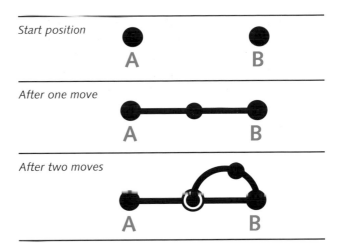

Start position

After one move

After two moves

End of game

Advanced game

Once you've got the hang of the simple version, try starting the game with three or four unconnected dots.

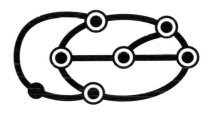

Off to work we go

Workers from the electricity, gas, water, and telephone companies need to get to their corresponding offices. However, so suspicious are they of their rivals that they will not even cross the path taken by any of the other employees. Can you lead each employee to the correct office without any of their paths crossing?

Upsizing

Suppose, instead, there were six workers trying to get to six offices. Would the problem still be solvable?

ANSWERS page 91

ROADS AND TREES

The council of the small island of Fifetons is in disarray. None of the counselors can agree on how many essentially different road schemes they have to consider. They could be here all week. Thankfully, help is close at hand...

Ground plan

A counselor from the nearby island of Fawrtons had come along to Fifetons' planning meeting. "We drew out all the essentially different possibilities," explained the counselor. "Each one had a unique way of connecting up the roads, no matter how the roads were laid out in real life. We found there were 16 ways of connecting together four towns using just three roads. Although you have five towns, to be connected with four roads, that should help." Indeed it did. Can you work out how many essentially different plans the Roads Committee of Fifetons will have to consider?

HINT It is a powerful series, and examining simpler examples may be useful.

ANSWER page 91

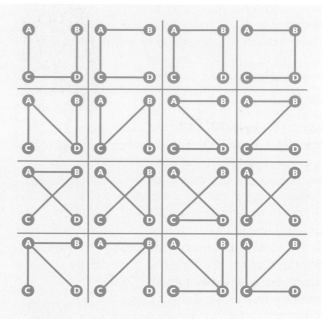

Lang time, no see

On the nearby Lang Island, there are also four towns but they are spaced farther apart, as shown. The position of each town is accurate. The previous road system was scrapped, and it is currently not possible for anyone to travel anywhere safely. What arrangement of roads will allow access to every town and yet use the shortest total length of road?

HINT The roads can cross and form junctions if you wish.

ANSWER page 91

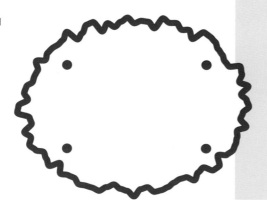

? Did you know...

The problem of visiting all four towns in the shortest possible distance is called **The Traveling Salesman Problem.** It is not straightforward to work out the shortest route to take. Imagine this with more towns and roads, and the calculations rapidly increase. If a salesman had a 50-city itinerary, even a fast computer would take 1,000,000,000,000,000,000,000, 000,000,000,000,000 times the age of the universe to calculate the best route. This kind of puzzle, in which the possibilities increase rapidly when the problem gets only slightly more complex, is known as a **non-deterministic polynomial (NP) problem.**

Mathematical trees

Trees are traditional symbols of life and growth. Tree graphs occur in early attempts to represent logical relations diagrammatically, and they were known to Aristotle. Ancient and medieval philosophers were obsessed with tree graphs. These are still widely used to classify objects in hierarchical systems. For example, the classification of all living creatures is broken down into kingdoms, which branch into phyla, genera, species, and so on.

A related area of mathematics in which topological ideas arise is the theory of graphs. When nodes are joined by lines, what matters is not the precise **position** of the lines and nodes but **the way they connect**. A graph is **connected** if it is all in one piece, meaning that there is a continuous path from any node to any other. The precise shape of the edges is irrelevant.

If a graph contains a **circuit** (that is, any closed loop of different lines), then so does any topologically equivalent graph. Graphs that do not contain any circuits are called **trees**. It is easy to see why—the lines often branch but they never link up again.

Many real-life processes can be represented as trees. For example, Connect Four, the "drop counters to get four in a row" game, has been so thoroughly analyzed by a computer mapping out the entire tree of possible moves that the computer cannot lose. Chess has not been "solved" in this way because the possible routes multiply rapidly after just a few moves.

A **binary tree,** in which a maximum of two branches occur at any node, is a basic form of artificial intelligence. Examples of binary tree guessing games can be found on the Internet. For example, the computer may invite you to think of a sitcom character. It will then ask you a series of yes/no questions such as "Are you thinking of a man?" and "Are you thinking of an American character?" Depending on your answer, the computer goes down a different branch of the tree. At the very end of any particular path, the computer will say which character you are thinking of.

If your choice doesn't agree with the computer's suggestion, you can add a new question that distinguishes between the character you were thinking of and the computer's guess. This adds another node and branch to the tree, which means that the tree has "learned" a new person. Over time, the tree grows and increases the chance of guessing the right answer. Another fun thing to do is to play the tree again, answering the questions as you would personally—the result tells you which sitcom character you most closely resemble.

Points	Trees	Points	Trees
2		7	
3			
4			
5			
6			

THE GAME OF TREES

The idea of topological equivalence is fundamental to many areas of modern mathematics. This is a simple and rewarding game for two or more players, designed to encourage such understanding.

Set-up

On pages 101 and 103, you will find diagrams depicting a selection of 64 tree graphs with 3, 4, 5, and 6 nodes, which you can cut out. If you are playing with the **Advanced rule** (see below), note that each of the 16 rows contain 4 topologically equivalent cards (i.e., their endpoints and junctions are essentially the same except for rotations).

You will also need a set of six sticks of the same length (such as pencils, chopsticks) to re-create the graphs shown on the cards.

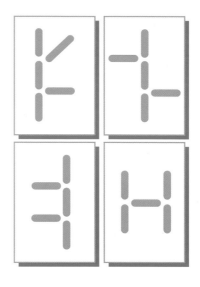

CARDS FOR PLAYING TREES

Here are four graphs that all have six endpoints. They are all topologically equivalent.

Rules of the game

Object

To collect the highest score by using the sticks to form the graphs shown on the cards.

How to play

1 Shuffle the cards and place them facedown in a pile.
2 Place five sticks in a straight line on the table. The sixth stick is held in reserve.
3 The first player takes the top three cards from the pile and places them face up. He or she then has **two** moves (types of move explained opposite) to change the positions of the sticks to match the graphs shown on the exposed cards.
4 If a player succeeds in forming such a graph, he or she takes that card and keeps it until the end of the game. **Note:** A player may take a card even if the sticks are in a different orientation to that on the card. For example, if the sticks look correct when the card is turned upside down, the player wins the card.
5 The second player now takes enough cards from the pile to bring the number of exposed cards up to three once more, and plays in exactly the same way.
6 Each person keeps taking turns to play until all the cards have been taken.

Valid moves

There are three basic types of move:
A Pick up one stick from the line of sticks on the table and lay it in a new position.
B Add a stick from the reserve.
C Remove a stick and place it in reserve. On his or her turn, a player can make any two moves plus as many **free moves** (rotations, see below) as desired.
D A player may make a **rotation** at any time. A rotation involves pivoting a stick about one of its ends, provided this end remains attached to the remainder of the graph at all times. Clearly, a stick that is attached at both ends cannot rotate.

There is no limit to the number of rotations a player may make. If the player achieves a target shape after one or more rotations, he or she wins that card.

Winning

The winner is the player with the most cards.

Advanced rule

In the advanced version, a player may also take a card if the graph on the card is topologically equivalent to the current orientation of the sticks.

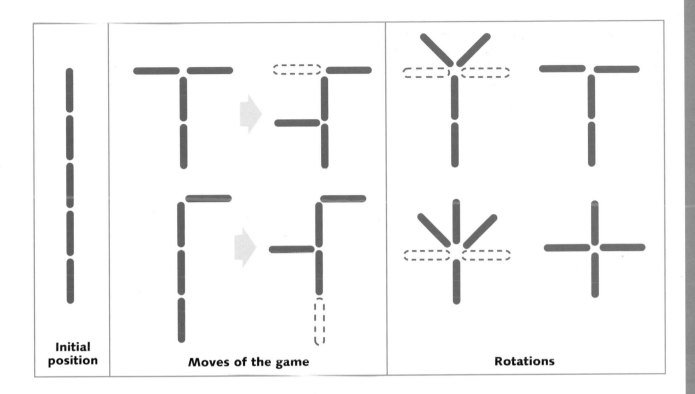

| Initial position | Moves of the game | Rotations |

Sample move

It is the first player's turn. The five sticks are placed in a straight line, with the sixth in reserve. The top row shows the three cards that the first player turned up. **Note:** In this example we are playing the game without the use of the **Advanced rule**.

FIRST MOVE Player moves one stick (move type **A**) and rotates one other (free move type **D**) to achieve diagram 3. Take that card.

FREE MOVE Player rotates the bottom stick for free (move type **D**) and wins card 1, even though the graph is upside-down.

SECOND MOVE Player returns one stick to the reserve (move type **C**) and wins card 2.

Therefore, this player has scored all three available points. The next player now turns over three new cards and the game continues.

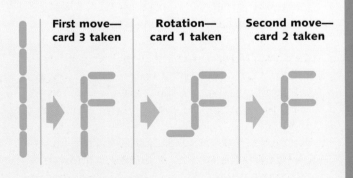

First move— card 3 taken   Rotation— card 1 taken   Second move— card 2 taken

RAMSEY'S GAME

Some theorems about graphs with identifiable nodes and lines were proved by Frank Plumpton Ramsey, so this graph-coloring game is named after him. Here the game board is a nine-node **complete graph**—that is, every node is connected to every other node.

Ramsey's game
Equipment needed
1 Two felt-tip pens (preferably the type that draw on acetate overhead projector sheets) of different colors
2 One sheet of transparent acetate

How to play
Two players (red and blue in this example) take turns to color one complete line (node to node) on the board. However, you may not draw a line if it forms a closed triangle whose edges are all the same color.

Winning
The first player who finds it impossible to make a valid move is the loser. The other player is the winner.

Follow-up activity
Try playing the game with other complete graphs.

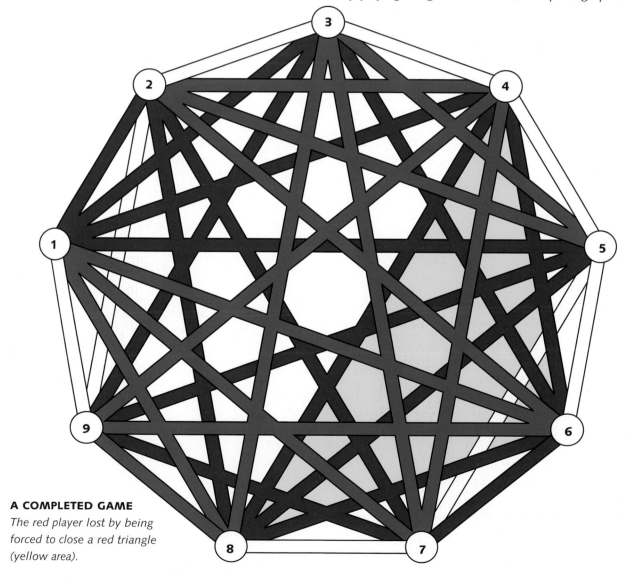

A COMPLETED GAME
The red player lost by being forced to close a red triangle (yellow area).

RAMSEY'S GAME

Ramsey game board

Place a transparent plastic sheet over this page, so that you can play the game several times without marking the book (or see **cutout** on page 105).

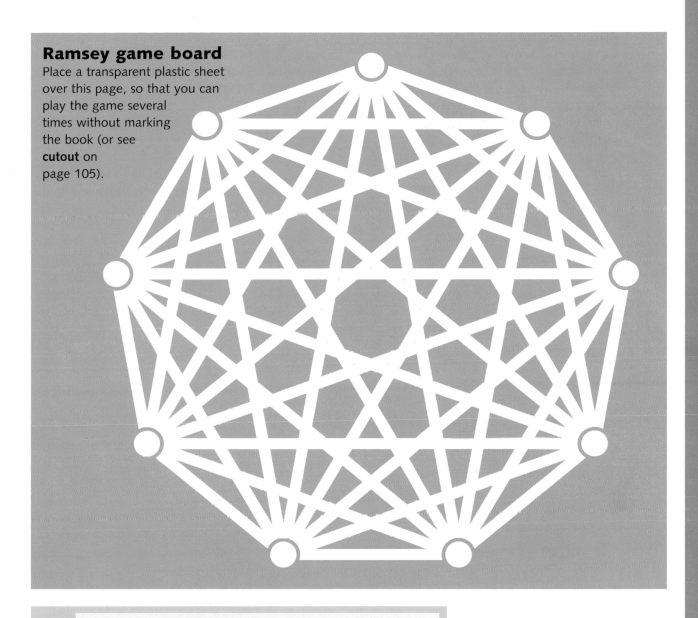

? Who was...Ramsey?

The mathematician and philosopher Frank Plumpton Ramsey was born in Cambridge, England, in 1903. He read mathematics at Trinity College there, and was only 21 years old when he was made a fellow of King's College. He was inspired by Bertrand Russell—another famous mathematician and philosopher, who proved that all mathematics was logic and nothing else. Ramsey died at the early age of 26 following surgery.

INGENIOUS TANGRAMS

4

DISSECTIONS

In Chinese, the tangram is called "the ingenious puzzle of seven pieces," but no one is quite sure how the puzzle was originally devised. The prolific American puzzler Sam Loyd claimed that historians had discovered 4000-year-old scriptures of the god Tan, but this was a cheeky hoax. Others believe that mathematicians devised the puzzle many hundreds of years ago. However, it is difficult to find any concrete proof of its existence until the 18th century. Whatever the true story, the puzzle only became popular in about 1800 after Western sailors and traders brought it back from their trips to the port of Canton in China.

The tangram consists of seven regular geometric-shaped pieces, cut from a square, which are used to form silhouettes of hundreds of different figures. They resemble people, animals, geometrical designs, and everyday objects.

Unlike jigsaw puzzles, in which the required assembly is unique due to the interlocking nature of the pieces, tangram puzzles offer few clues to the solver. A combination of spatial awareness, trial and error, and playing on hunches is necessary to crack the most difficult problems.

There are dozens of variations on the tangram, but here we present it in its original form, probably still the best puzzle of its type.

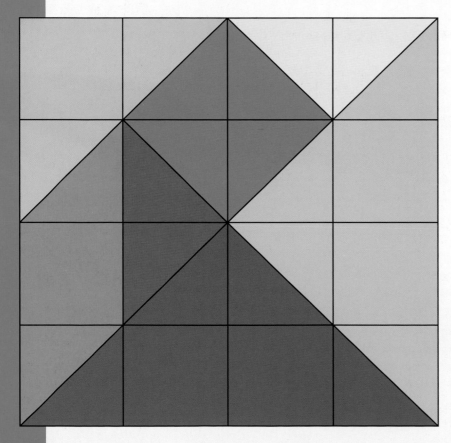

How to make a tangram

To make your own tangram, **cut out** the top seven pieces on page 107. Now try to do some of the puzzles on the opposite page.

Tangram challenges

Using the tangram pieces, try to form each of these
pictures. There are only two rules: All seven pieces
must be used, and the pieces are not allowed to
overlap. Start off with the people and animals first,
then move on to the more difficult geometric designs.

ANSWERS page 91

INGENIOUS TANGRAMS

For this puzzle, cut out the two identical sets of pieces on page 107. Take the four largest triangles and arrange them as shown in either of the diagrams below. Now use all the remaining pieces to complete the large square. Once you've solved one, try the other.

DOUBLE TANGRAM PUZZLE

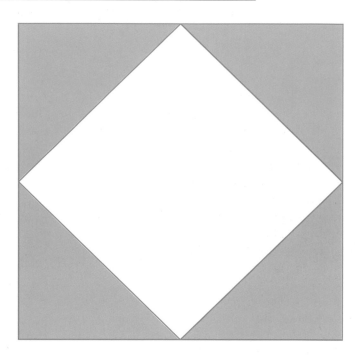

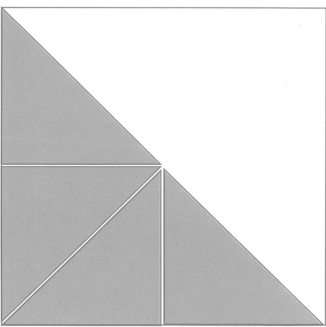

ANSWER page 91

ABOUT THE SQUARE

What's so great about squares? Mathematicians, magicians, and people who like puzzles and games get very excited about them because they are simple and complete, but also because they are shapes you can do much with. The author Lewis Carroll's opinion was clear:

RECTANGULAR! IT'S A SQUARE! BEAUTIFUL & EQUILATERAL!

A square is defined as a plane figure with four equal sides and four right (90°) angles. A square is counted as a rectangle, but is regarded as a special type. If the length of the side of a square is **X**, then the area of the square is **X** to the power of **2**, or **X** squared. This is where the term for the product that results from multiplying anything by itself comes from.

When a square is divided into smaller squares we obtain a **matrix** or **lattice** that becomes **magic** when filled with numbers in special configurations. In its lifelong partnership with the right-angled triangle, the square has inspired more mathematics than most of us are aware exist. From Pythagoras' Theorem to Einstein's General Theory of Relativity, and from the flat geometry of Euclid to the curvature of space, it is but

three or four short steps, with the square as their common thread.

The Pythagoreans called four, the first non-trivial square number, the number of justice, because it is the first one obtained by multiplying the same number together: 2 x 2 = 4. To this day, square means "truth." Someone who is a **square shooter** or is **foursquare** is a frank and honest person with firm convictions. A **square meal** is good, honest food, while President Theodore Roosevelt offered his citizens the **Square Deal** in 1902.

The square is found in nature in the crystals of many minerals, including common salt (sodium chloride). It has provided the proportions for famous ancient structures and modern buildings and even played a role in the structure of the Hebrew alphabet.

The square has given birth to many ancient games that are still played today: chess, Go, solitaire, dominoes—and many new games that have yet to be created. Try your hand at the square activities overleaf.

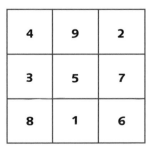

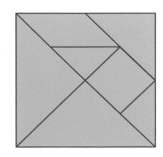

4	9	2
3	5	7
8	1	6

VARIATIONS ON THE SQUARE

SPLITTING SQUARES

Jigsaws are named after the workshop tool used to create them. See if you can crack these devious jigsaws. Use cardboard and the **cutouts** on page 109 to make them yourself.

Square dissections

All these patterns can be made by drawing a square, then dividing the sides into halves or thirds. They can easily be drawn, colored, and cut out to become dissection puzzles (see **cut-out** on page 109).

To re-create the original squares from their parts is often harder than you might think...

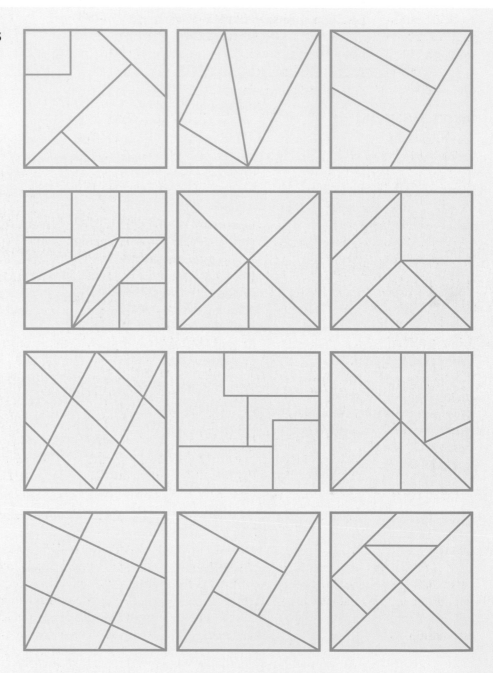

Five-piece suite

This five-piece jigsaw is very versatile. To make one, draw a square, then mark the point that is halfway along each edge. Then draw a diagonal line from one corner to the middle of an opposite side, as shown. Now cut out the pieces **along the solid black lines** in the illustration to give you five pieces (or see **cutout** on page 111).

In succession, rearrange the five parts to form the five geometrical figures shown on the right.

1 rectangle
2 triangle
3 Swiss cross
4 parallelogram
5 rhomboid

ANSWER page 91

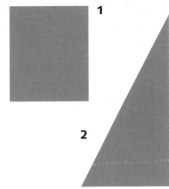
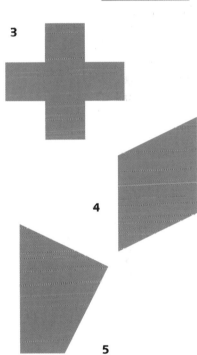

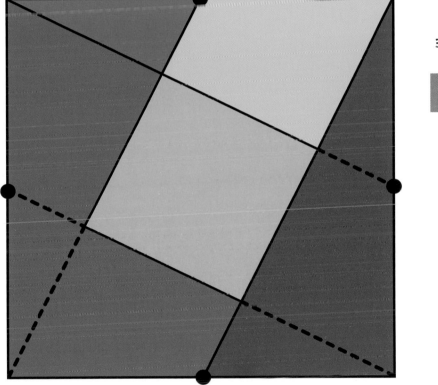

Squarea

Suppose the area of the overall square in the **Five-piece suite** puzzle is 100 square units. What is the area of the individual small square piece?

ANSWER page 91

Number jig

Suppose you had a jigsaw consisting of 1,000 standard (interlocking) pieces. Joining one group of pieces to one other group of pieces counts as one move. Here, a group means one or more. What is the fewest number of moves that it will take to connect all 1,000 pieces? What is the greatest number of moves required?

ANSWER page 91

REARRANGEMENTS

Hexagon to triangle puzzle

Copy and cut out the six parts of the dissected hexagon (or see **cutout** on page 111). Rearrange the six parts to form an equilateral triangle. Pieces may be flipped over if necessary.

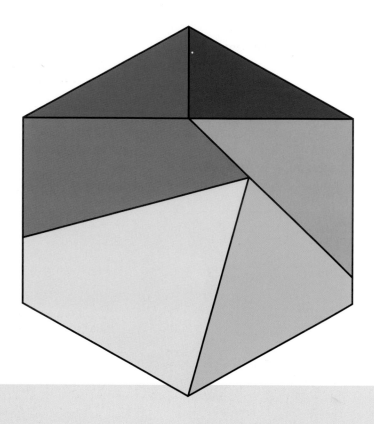

ANSWER page 91

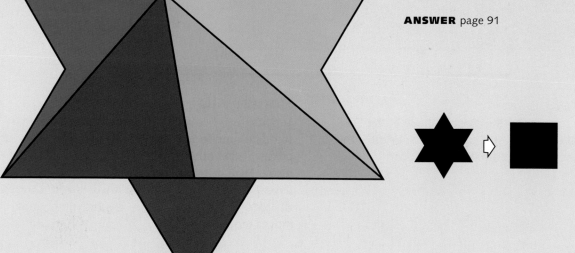

Six-pointed star puzzle

Copy and cut out the six parts of the dissected six-pointed star (or see **cutout** on page 111). Rearrange the six parts to form a perfect square.

ANSWER page 91

Stars puzzle

Copy and cut out the 24 parts of the 12-pointed star (or see **cutout** on page 111). Rearrange the 24 pieces to form three identically shaped smaller replicas of the big star.

ANSWER page 91

STORAGE ROOM

PACKING 'EM IN 5

Ashia was attempting to de-junk her life. After years of collecting thimbles, pottery pigs, and countless back issues of *Barbie World* magazine, but without the heart to throw them out, she decided to pack the lot off to be looked after by the Fair and Square Storage Company (FASSC).

The company supplies free cubic cardboard boxes for its customers to use. Unusually, the firm charges by the amount of floor space the boxes take up, and insists that the area must be square. So if you don't use all of your area, that's tough luck. However, the length of the square's sides does not have to be a whole number. Incidentally, boxes cannot be stacked on top of each other for safety reasons.

When Ashia sent her first storage box to FASSC, she was charged one unit. When she had another box to send, she soon realized that she might as well send two more because the cost would be the same for two, three, or four boxes (2 x 2).

When the fifth box was full, things got a bit more complicated. Since there was no reason why the boxes couldn't be tilted, clever solutions were possible. Out of the two likely possibilities, the more efficient packing was obtained if only the central square was tilted. In this instance, the cost was 2.707 units because that was the size of the smallest square that contained all the boxes.

The next tricky decision came when the amount of junk stored reached ten boxes (yes, Ashia liked Barbie that much). No one has yet found a better solution than the one shown, but that doesn't mean one doesn't exist. For the eleventh and final box, FASCC was going to charge Ashia for 3.914 units of storage. However, a slightly better solution was possible…

BOXING CLEVER

How Ashia's belongings from one to eleven boxes were packed in the warehouse.

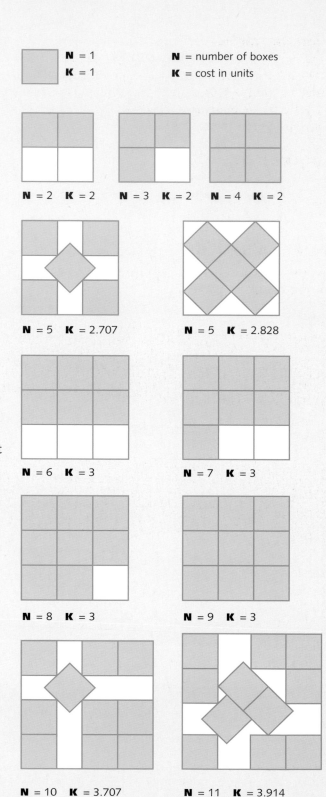

N = 1
K = 1

N = number of boxes
K = cost in units

N = 2 K = 2 N = 3 K = 2 N = 4 K = 2

N = 5 K = 2.707 N = 5 K = 2.828

N = 6 K = 3 N = 7 K = 3

N = 8 K = 3 N = 9 K = 3

N = 10 K = 3.707
(best packing known so far)

N = 11 K = 3.914
(not the minimal)

Boxing clever

Cut out 11 unit squares of exactly the dimensions shown below. The aim of the game is to pack all the squares into the square warehouse below. Remember that no square must cross the black line nor overlap any other square. It can be done!

ANSWER page 92

Did you know...

This type of packing problem was important in the days when wars were won with cannon fire. By using a telescope to determine the packing pattern and height of your opponents' pile of cannonballs, you could determine how much ammunition they had left.

PACKING FLOOR AREA

K = 3.877

UNIT SQUARE

PAVING THE WAY

Terry Cotta is the proud owner of "Terry's Mad Mad Mad Mad Mad Mad Tile and Paving Warehouse," the brand new out-of-town emporium for all your tile and paving needs. Terry stocks only square tiles in unit sizes because he feels they are usable for any purpose—you can see some of his impressive shop displays, made out of squares, on the opposite page.

Patio ratio

Suppose a customer came in to Terry's Mad Mad Mad … shop to buy some tiles for a square patio. The customer wants to use at least two paving slabs. Since Terry stocks only square shapes in various sizes, as shown below, what is the fewest number of square slabs the customer will need to buy? In other words, what is the smallest number of squares you can divide these squares into? We have provided grids for areas of 2 x 2 up to 13 x 13.

ANSWER page 92

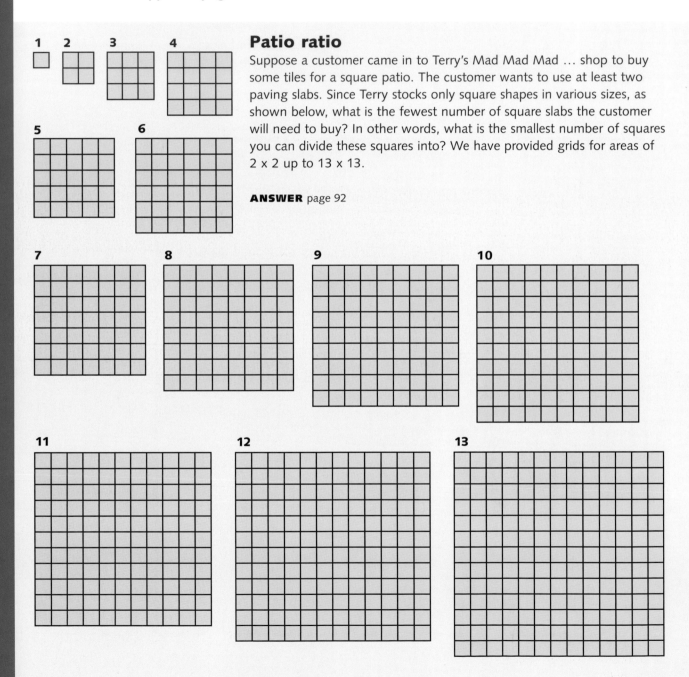

PAVING THE WAY

TERRY'S TILES
*Some attractive designs formed from
squares only.*

DRAWN, HALVED, AND QUARTERED

Mr. and Mrs. Moore's terrible twins, Polly and Molly, were always arguing. Whether it was the number of Rice Krispies in their breakfast bowls or who had the most glittery makeup, nothing was beyond their squabbles.

So when the Moore family moved into their new designer home, mayhem was about to break loose. Mr. Moore had decided to divide each room into two, so that each child could play on her own without argument. The rather freeform design of the rooms meant that this was going to be a bit tricky, however...

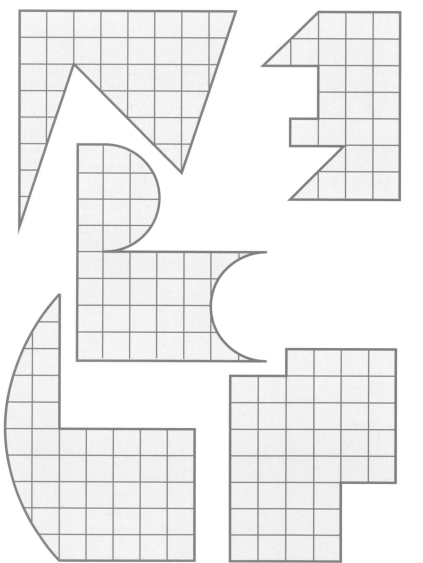

Separate the sisters

How can Mr. Moore divide each of these rooms into two so that each twin has the same play area? The sisters insist that areas must be exactly **congruent**—that is, the same shape as well as the same area. Mr. Moore wants to draw just one line across each room, although he doesn't mind whether the line is straight or curved. Incidentally, the square grid might help but doesn't have to be followed.

ANSWER page 92

Did you know...
A half and a quarter are the only two fractions with special names. All the other names (a third, fifth, sixth, seventh...) are the same as the ordinal numbers.

DRAWN, HALVED, AND QUARTERED

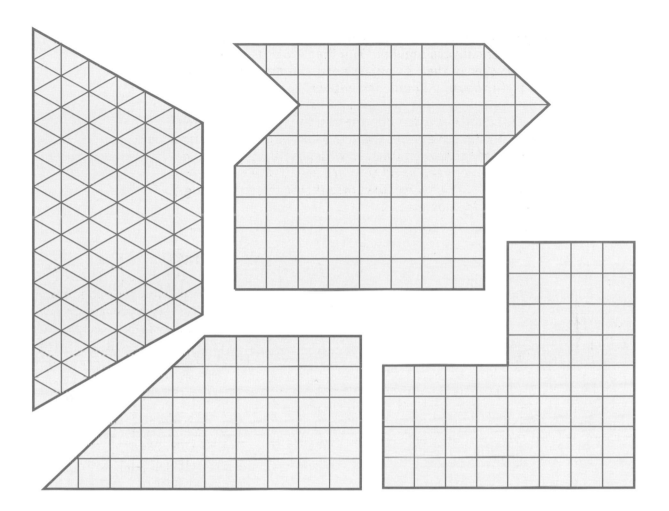

Sequestrate the siblings

Happily (or sadly, depending on how you look at it)
Mrs. Moore gave birth to two bouncing baby boys
some years later. They moved to a house with rooms
that were larger and, thankfully, less esoteric in
shape. Yet even now none of the children were
getting on with each other. How can Mr. Moore
divide each of these rooms into four using the
same conditions as the previous puzzle so that Polly,
Molly, Tommy, and Timmy all have identical areas
in which to play?

ANSWER page 92

Did you know...
The **half-life** of some radioactive
material is the amount of time it
takes for its mass to decay to half its
original value. If you were to plot a
graph of the mass over time,
it would be smooth and gradually
become more horizontal—this is
known as an **exponential curve**.
The half-life of a radioactive
material can vary wildly—the isotope
polonium-212 halves in under a
microsecond while uranium-236
takes 4,500,000,000 years to do
the same.

POLYGO

6

JIGSAWS

The earliest jigsaw puzzle is said to have been invented by Englishman John Spilsbury in about 1760. He intended it to be used as an educational toy, but jigsaws are still used by adults, including Queen Elizabeth II, as a pastime, especially over Christmas. The next few pages offer you the opportunity to make a number of colorful jigsaws and jigsaw games for yourself, ranging from the simple to the virtually impossible.

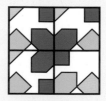

GAME SAMPLE
The four tiles in the center form a violet shape scoring 14 points.

Polygo

This puzzle game for two or more players is based on the recognition of polygons.

Set-up

Cut out all 24 squares on page 113. Lay the tiles facedown and mix them thoroughly.

How to play

1 Each player chooses a different color.
2 Players take turns to select a tile and place it face up on the table adjacent to the tiles already laid. The aim is to create polygons of the same color (see the game sample).
3 The game continues until all the tiles have been used.

Scoring

Each player adds up the scores of the completed polygons of their color. Each polygon will be formed from four tiles, placed in a square, with the four touching corners all having the same color. The point values for the scoring polygons are shown in the chart on the right. Shapes that differ only by a rotation still score.

Winning

The player with the highest total wins.

SCORE CARD

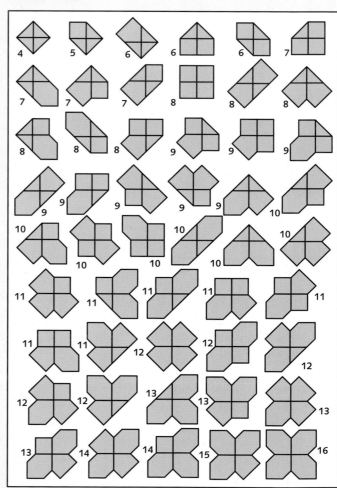

Solo version

You can also play a solitaire version of the game. Can you assemble all 24 tiles in a 6 x 4 rectangle so that all the colors match when two tiles are adjacent?

BITS AND PIECES

Ernie Flamsteed had been working in the depot of Awkward and Sons since 1937. Never one to be at the white hot tip of technology, he had only just started getting the hang of ordinary bar codes when along came a new invention—two-dimensional bar codes.

It stood to reason, his manager explained. Each tiny square represented a binary digit (or bit), which computers use to store data and as such are very flexible. This is why many companies were using them these days to store not just UPC (Universal Product Code) numbers but customer details and product descriptions, too. Admittedly, this new system required a more accurate form of reader. Ernie put on his brown coat and shuffled off down the corridor to see what all the fuss was about...

Bits jigsaw

This particular bar code system uses four squares. Since each square has two different possibilities (turquoise and blue), there are 2 x 2 x 2 x 2 = 16 different possibilities. Each possibility represents a number, and in turn several of these squares together can represent anything you like—symbols, words, pictures...

Make your own set of Bits pieces (see **cut-out** on page 115) then tackle the next puzzle and game.

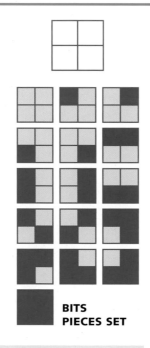

BITS PIECES SET

Ernie's enigma

Ernie was taking the inventory in the depot when he realized someone had stuck a permanent label right in the middle of the bar codes. Luckily, Ernie knows that each bar code can be constructed with a set of Bits pieces (see left). He could just see the edge of each bar code beneath the label, so that helped. Furthermore, the colors of adjacent 2 x 2 Bits pieces match on all edges. Can you reassemble the bar codes so that they are valid for all 6 products. (see **cut-out** on page 115)?

ANSWER page 92

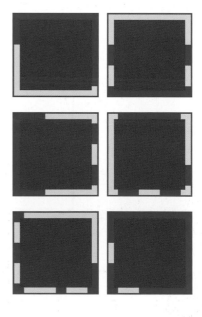

Did you know . . .

The first supermarket product to be scanned by bar code was a packet of Wrigley's chewing gum. The momentous event happened on June 26, 1974, at the Marsh Supermarket in Troy, Ohio. The pack of gum is currently held in the Smithsonian Institution, Washington, D.C. The first patent for a bar code dates back to 1949, and bar codes were used in the early 1960s to identify railway rolling stock.

Bits board game

The Bits pieces you made for the previous puzzle can also be used for this engaging two-player game. Ernie finds it a gentle diversion when life in the depot gets too hectic for him.

Set-up

You need one set of 16 Bits tiles and the 8 x 8 square board below (see page 115) such that each tile fits exactly on four of its squares. Place the tiles face down and mix them thoroughly.

How to play

1 In turn, each player must take a tile and place it on the board. It must fit over exactly four of the squares on the board.

2 Whenever a tile is played, it must match the edges of any adjacent tiles already on the board, in a fashion similar to dominos.

3 Tiles may be placed so that they touch only half an edge of another tile—see the sample game below.

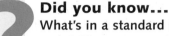

Did you know...

What's in a standard stripey bar code? There are a pair of bars at the left, middle, and right of the pattern that warn the reader that a bar code is imminent. A laser then reads two sets of numbers—the set on the left is usually the code number of the manufacturer. The second set is the actual product number. There is also a "check digit"—a precalculated number that gives the reader a 90% chance of ensuring it has read the bar code correctly, and that the width of the bar codes hasn't been tampered with.

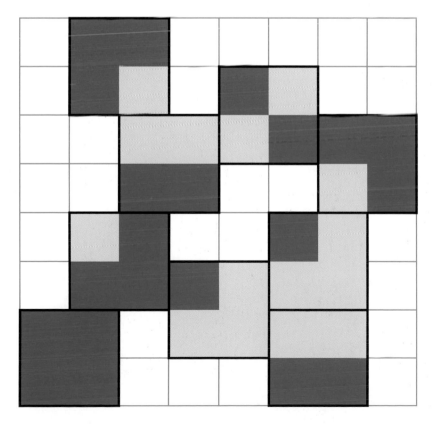

Winning

The first player unable to place his or her tile is the loser. The other player wins.

Open exercise

What is the shortest possible game you can find? That is, if a single player plays solitaire, and selects from the 16 tiles laid face up, what is the smallest number of tiles needed to block the board so that no others can be laid?

ANSWER page 92

BITS BOARD GAME SAMPLE
This game was completed in nine moves.

HONEYCOMBS AND HEXABITS

There are only three types of tiles made from regular polygons that can **tessellate**—that is, cover an infinitely large wall without leaving any gaps. They are triangles, squares, and hexagons. Bees obviously plumped for the last option when designing their honeycombs.

Hexabits

The set of hexagons shown here represent different ways of dividing a hexagon into two-color areas. Copy and cut out all 19 shapes (see **cut-out** on page 117). The object of the game is to fit all the hexagons onto the blank honeycomb grid opposite so that all touching edges match in color.

Hexabits puzzle
Place all 19 pieces on this grid. Remember to match the color of all touching edges.

ANSWER page 92

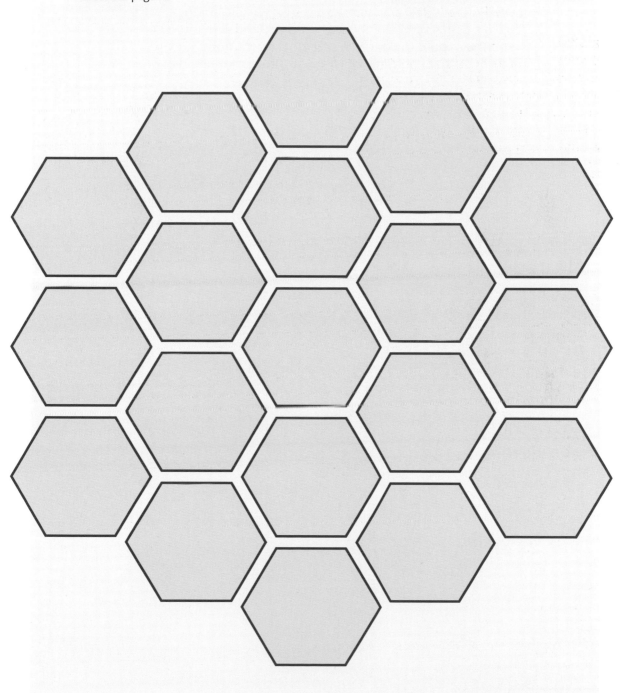

DIY DOMINOES

Grandpa Wilkins had done it again. "Hang on, I've just found the double five." Never the most organized of people, he left his domino set all over the room. After searching for an hour with only nine discovered dominoes to show for their efforts, his nephews were becoming impatient. Luckily, the eldest nephew—a bit of a whiz at math—realized that by using some cardboard, scissors, and a few colored pens they could make some rather different dominoes of their own that could prove to be far more challenging.

Domino derby

To play this combination puzzle, copy out the 24 colored square dominoes (see **cut-out** on page 119). These show every possible way of coloring a square's edges using three colors. The aim of the game is to make all the dominoes fit so that all the touching edges match. This in itself is not too difficult. The extra twist is that the entire outer border must be the same color.

ANSWER page 92

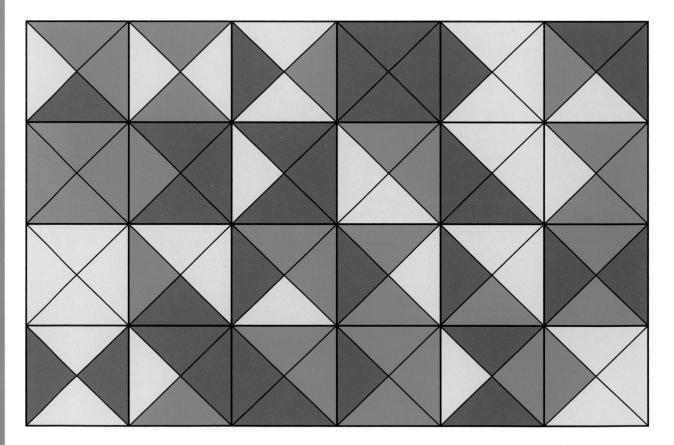

DIY DOMINOES

Domino rally

Cut out the 24 triangular dominoes on page 119. Again, the touching edges must match and the entire outer border of the hexagonal grid must be the same color.

ANSWER page 92

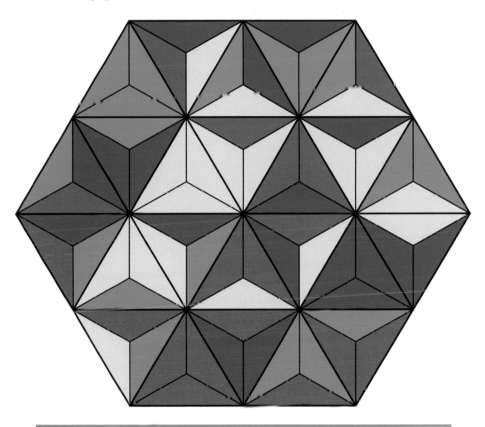

How many bones?

How many domino pieces, or "bones," are there in a traditional (standard) set? Can you get the answer by reasoning rather than simply listing them all?

ANSWER page 92

? Did you know...
Traditional dominoes didn't have blanks originally and were used in 12th-century China to represent all throws possible with two dice. The Chinese called them dotted cards. They were introduced into England by French prisoners in the late 18th century. Some North American Inuits play a similar game to dominos using sets of up to 148 pieces.

LO-SHU AND FRIENDS

Magic Squares are one of the oldest and most popular puzzles in existence. It is thought that the first magic square, the Lo-Shu, dates from as early as 2200 BC. It appeared in the *Chinese Book of Permutations*.

The magic square is a set of natural numbers (positive integers) in serial order, beginning with 1, arranged in a square formation, with the following magic property: If you add the numbers in any row or any column, or either of the main diagonals, you always get the same result, called the "magic number."

The Lo-shu magic square

There is only one way of forming a magic square from the whole numbers from 1 to 9 inclusive. Can you find it?

ANSWER page 92

A diabolic square

Albrecht Dürer's etching *Melancholia* includes this 4 x 4 magic square. We've removed all the odd numbers from the diagram. Can you replace them to complete it? When you've done that, see how many ways you can obtain the magic number 34 from the solution.

ANSWER page 93

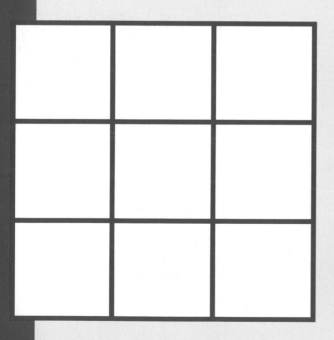

Latin square of order 5

Leonhard Euler devised a new type of magic square, the Latin square, in which no color appears more than once in any direction, horizontally, vertically, or on the two main diagonals. As a puzzle, see if you can place the colors in a suitable Latin square arrangement.

ANSWER page 93

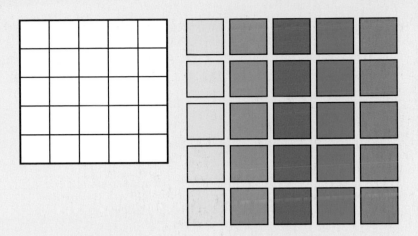

Latin square of order 6

This time, the aim of the puzzle is to create a Latin square of order 6. Is this possible? Can you place 32 tiles on the board?

ANSWER page 93

Latin square game

If you have a friend with you, you can play a game using the concepts covered in the puzzles above. First, make 25 tiles (five of each of five colors). Players alternate by placing a tile on the 5 x 5 game board so that no color appears more than once in any row, column, or diagonal. Once a tile is placed on the board, it cannot be moved. The winner is the last player able to make a valid move.

Once you've mastered this game, make a few more pieces to bring your set up to six pieces in six colors and play the game on the 6 x 6 grid using the same rules.

NOT FAIR AND SQUARE

See if you can crack these more advanced magic square problems.

The tricky eight

In the Lo-Shu puzzle on page 54, you will have found that the 8 normally occupies one of the corner spaces. Can you make a magic square in which the magic number is 15 and the 8 is placed in the position shown? You can use any numbers you like.

ANSWER page 93

In the red

Complete this magic square so that it contains nine consecutive integer numbers. Seems easy, doesn't it?

ANSWER page 93

NOT FAIR AND SQUARE

Versatile squares

Not all magic squares have to be about adding up numbers:

A How could you distribute the whole numbers from 1 to 9 inclusive in a 3 x 3 grid so that when you subtract the middle number from the sum of the outer two numbers in any row, column, or main diagonal, the result is always the same?

B How could you distribute 1, 2, 3, 4, 6, 9, 12, 18, and 36 so that the numbers in any row, column, and main diagonal give the same product if multiplied?

c How could you distribute the numbers 1, 2, 3, 4, 6, 9, 12, 18, and 36 so that, for any row, column, and main diagonal of three numbers, the following always gives the same result: (outer two numbers multiplied together) divided by (central number)?

ANSWER page 93

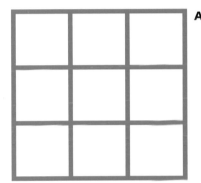 A

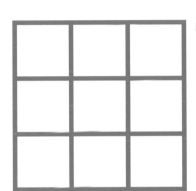 B

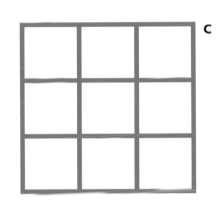 C

Devilish dozen

If anything, this is a non-magic diagram. The aim is to place the numbers from 1 to 12 into the grid so that no two consecutive numbers appear **anywhere** in the same row, column, or any of the diagonals.

ANSWER page 93

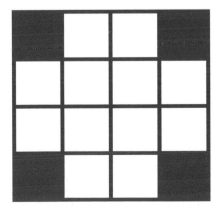

That's odd

Place the odd numbers 1, 3, 5,…21, 23, 25 into the remaining cells to form a standard magic square.

ANSWER page 93

14	10		22	18
20				24
2				6
8	4		16	12

LIFE'S A LOTTERY

You may know that the odds in a lottery of picking the winning 6 balls from the numbers 1 to 49 are around 14 million to 1, but where does this number come from? There are 49 possibilities for the first ball, 48 for the second, 47 for the third, and so on until 44 for the sixth. So that's 49 x 48 x 47 x 46 x 45 x 44. But remember that the order of the six winning balls does not matter. By a similar token, there are 6 x 5 x 4 x 3 x 2 x 1 ways of arranging those balls. Dividing this number into the original result gives 13,983,816 different results, or permutations.

Using the factorial notation we've already encountered in this book in the answer to the **Runes** puzzle on page 22, where $n! = n \times (n-1) \times ... \times 3 \times 2 \times 1$, you could write this as $49!/(43! \times 6!)$.

Tiles for Permutino

There are $4! = 4 \times 3 \times 2 \times 1 = 24$ ways of coloring a strip of four squares using four colors once each. Practically, there only 12 different designs because you can turn any strip upside down to match another strip. Copy and cut out the 24 strips to play the Permutino game (see **cut-out** on page 121).

?

Did you know...

Spain is the world's most avid gambling nation. In El Gordo ("the fat one") up to 2.75 trillion pesetas (about $24.5 billion) are staked every year. Whole villages join together to buy sequential books of tickets—sometimes a big win can be shared throughout the neighborhood. One in three tickets wins some form of prize. In an effort to help handicapped people, Spanish lottery tickets are sold only by registered blind persons.

Permutino

This game for two to four players is based on the dominoes principle.

Set-up

You will need one set of 24 Permutino tiles. Deal the strips to players in turn, until all have been dealt.

How to play

1 Each player chooses a color.

2 Players take turns to add a strip to the pattern on the table. It must match the existing colors along all edges that touch.

3 If a player cannot lay a strip he forfeits his turn.

4 When all the strips have been laid, or no player can move, each player calculates his score.

Scoring

Any square belonging to a connected region of squares of a player's color that contains **four or more** squares counts as one point (so a four-square connection merits four points). In the example game shown, blue has seven points because he has a connected region with seven squares in it. In the event of a tie, the player with the largest connected region wins.

PERMUTINO GAME SAMPLE
Sample game with its score chart.

Color	Number of squares					
	8	7	6	5	4	Score
					▣	4
		▣				7
					▣	4
						4

Postman's knock

Every day, a postman has to deliver exactly one letter to each house in a street. The postman is rather demoralized, and does not bother to look at the address on each envelope, preferring to leave things to chance. Given that the number of houses does not matter, how many of the letters, on average, will be delivered to the correct destination?

ANSWER page 93

What are the odds?

Jessie has just sealed her Christmas cards into five different envelopes but has forgotten which card is addressed to whom. If she puts the five corresponding addresses on the envelopes at random, what is the probability that **A** all five envelopes are addressed correctly? **B** exactly four of the five envelopes are addressed correctly?

ANSWER page 93

WINDOW OF OPPORTUNITY

Bob Scratchitt was an expert in his chosen field of glassmaking. For the majority of his works, he used four different colors of glass, which were installed into small square arrangements. There were essentially six different arrangements, but by allowing rotations there were actually 24 varieties of tile available. This worked out very well, because Bob had just had an order for a new stained glass window from the Earl of Featherstonehaugh...

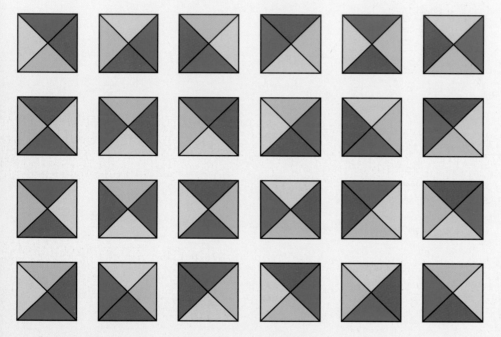

BOB'S SQUARE PANELS
There are six different designs in each of four rotations.

Window shield

Bob wants to fit all 24 of his stained glass panels into the window frame shown on the right. The middle square cannot be used because the Earl of Featherstonehaugh's coat of arms will go there later. All touching squares must share matching colors, domino-fashion. In addition, each outer edge of the window must have a single color, and there must be a different color for each edge. Make your own set of Bob's tiles (see **cut-out** on page 123) and use the 5 x 5 board on page 61. Can you satisfy Bob's demands?

ANSWER page 93

WINDOW OF OPPORTUNITY

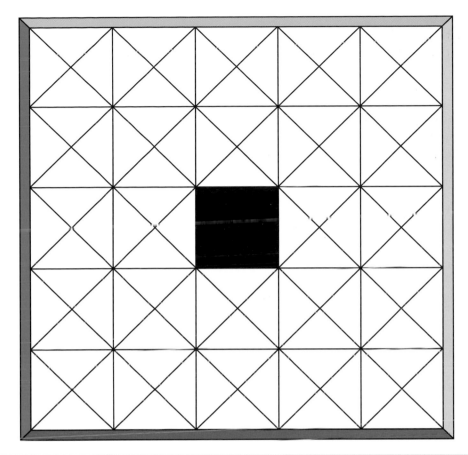

**STAINED GLASS
WINDOW FRAME**
*Fit the stained glass panels
in here.*

Square deal
This colorful domino game works best with two
players.

Set-up
You'll need a set of 24 square tiles and a 5 x 5 grid.
Lay the tiles facedown and mix them up.

How to play
1 The first player picks up a tile and places it
  anywhere on the board.
2 Players take turns playing a tile on the board.
  There are two rules: The tile you play must touch
  at least one previously played square, and all
  edges of neighboring tiles must match in color.

Winning
The first player unable to place his tile loses
the game.

Open exercise
What is the smallest number of tiles needed to block
the board so that no further play is possible with any
remaining tile?

?

Did you know...
Glass is sometimes considered
to be a liquid. The different
ingredients in the glass are in
a supercooled suspension, rather
than having the firm chemical bonds
of a usual solid. The different colors
of glass are obtained by adding
oxides of iron (red), copper (green),
or cobalt (blue).

PICTURE WINDOW

Bob Scratchitt (see pages 60–61) has recently diversified into hexagonal pieces of glass. By good fortune more than skill (by accidentally spilling a jar of metal filings), he's found that certain ingredients in his glass now allow a greater range of colors—six, to be precise.

If Bob can choose each color only once for each hexagon, then there are 6 x 5 x 4 = 120 raw combinations. However, a piece of glass can be rotated and turned over, which reduces the possibilities to the 20 different hexagons you see here.

Hexagons or cubes?

Bob has designed this window incorrectly—his 20 hexagon designs can't fit into the 19 available spaces shown on page 63. Can you mock up your own set of Bob's hexagonal tiles (see **cut-out** on page 125) and work out a way for any 19 of them to fit into the window frame? The edges of adjacent pieces must match colors. You'll understand the reasoning behind the title for this puzzle once you get going.

ANSWER page 94

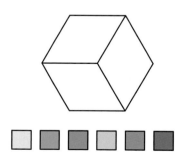

BOB'S HEXAGONAL TILES

Bob's new range of designs and colors.

PICTURE WINDOW

Window war

This game can be played with two or more players.

Set-up

You will need a set of 20 hexagonal pieces and the 19-space window grid shown on this page. Lay the tiles facedown and shuffle them.

How to play

1 Players take turns to pick a tile and place it anywhere on the board. (It does not need to be adjacent to an existing tile.)

2 If a player places a tile in such a way that it is adjacent to an existing piece, the touching edges must be the same color.

Winning

Anyone who cannot make a legal move has lost and must drop out of the game. They should replace their unplayed tile facedown in the reserve and mix it up with the others. Continue playing until there is only one person left—the winner.

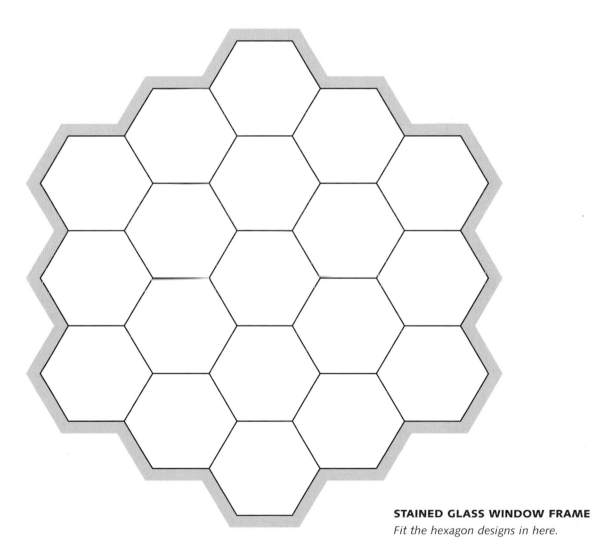

STAINED GLASS WINDOW FRAME
Fit the hexagon designs in here.

DISCO DISCOLORATION

Groovy Stu is very excited by his new business venture "Back 2 the 70s," a retro disco nightclub. "Tell me man, how do you want the floor panels?" hollered the chief workman fitting out the disco. "Chill, man," said Stu, "I've got a fabulicious design in mind. They don't call me Groovy Stu for nothing."

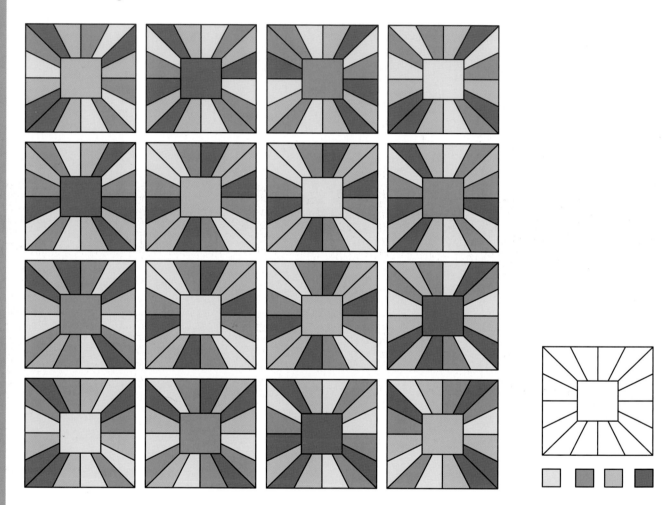

Dance floor dominoes

Here are the 16 square lighting panels Stu will be using for the floor of his nightclub. Arrange all 16 squares in a 4 x 4 array, obeying the domino principle—that is, all edges must match colors like for like. Use the square tile **cut-outs** on page 127.

HINT There is a better way to solve this than trial and error. Try to discover how the patterns work.

ANSWER page 94

DISCO DISCOLORATION

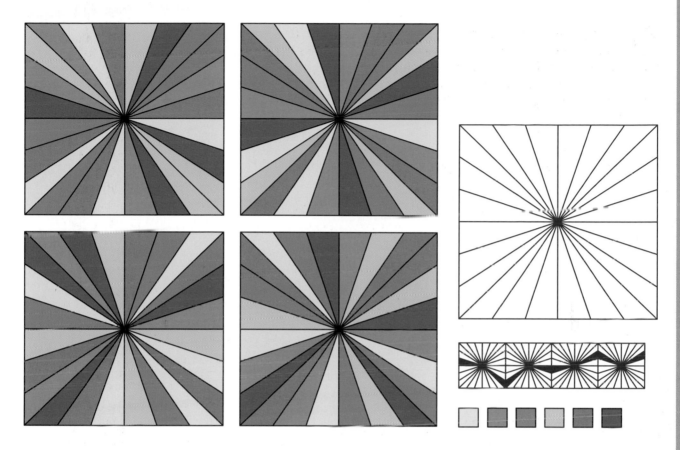

DJ display

These four lighting panels will be used behind the DJ booth. This time the sides of each square are colored using six different colors. The panels will be laid out in different ways so that it is possible to form a continuous zigzag line of the same color through the row of four squares (see small schematic). This can be done for five of the six colors. For which one of the six colors is this zigzag impossible? You may find it helpful to copy and color in your own version (see **cut-out** on page 127).

ANSWER page 94

Drive time

On Monday, Stu drove from his bachelor pad at 7:30 P.M. and arrived at the nightclub at 11:00 P.M. After a wild and crazy party, he left the nightclub on Tuesday night at 9:00 P.M. and (via a cab using the same route) arrived back home at 11:45 P.M. What are the chances that, at exactly the same time on Monday and Tuesday, Stu was at the same point along the road?

ANSWER page 94

VENERABLE BEADS

Jackie sells custom-built necklaces from her Internet web site, reallyreallynicenecklaces.com. Because her necklaces are so really, really nice, she receives orders from around the world. Customers can choose which configuration of beads they want—either all red, all yellow, or a specific mixture of the two.

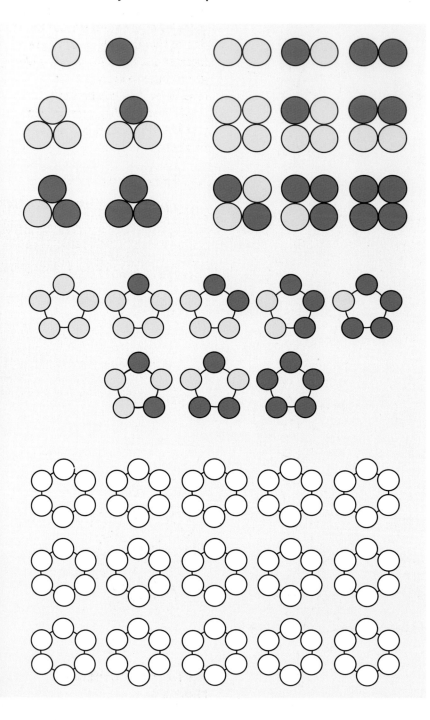

Sixth form

Jackie noticed during her work that the number of different designs was not obvious. Because necklaces can be rotated or turned over, many of the possible designs are not unique. The different designs achievable with up to five beads are shown. Use the blank diagram to work out how many are possible with six beads. You may not need to use all 15 diagrams.

ANSWER page 94

Guess what?

How many different necklace designs do you think Jackie could manufacture if each necklace were to contain a total of 20 beads in at most two colors? Don't work it out—just have a guess.

ANSWER page 94

THE NECKLACE-COLORING PROBLEM

VENERABLE BEADS

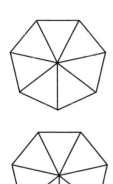

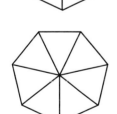

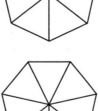

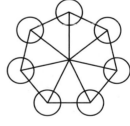

Seventh heaven

Johnny, Jackie's main competitor, sells jewelry through his web site, veryverygoodbrooches.com. His heptagonal designs are quite popular. Again, each of the seven triangles of each brooch can be one of two possible colors. How many brooch designs are possible given that the brooches are reversible (they can be turned over)? Use the diagrams to help you—some of them might not be needed.

ANSWER page 94

THE BROOCH-COLORING PROBLEM

KNIGHT, KNIGHT

9

MAKE YOUR MOVE

Chess has survived since the 6th century AD, and over the years chess pieces have been made in many forms and materials. Originally known as Chaturanga (the army game), chess spread to Europe some time between 700 and 900. In the Middle Ages, the game was played according to the Muslim rules wherein the queen and bishop were weaker than they are now because they could only move one square at a time.

In mathematical terms, chess is a "perfect information" game because both sides know everything about the opponent's position and how they reached it. (Compare this with poker, in which you don't know your opponent's cards.) This makes it much easier for people and computers to work out the best line of attack.

Did you know...
Chess has hit the headlines in recent years thanks to IBM's computer Deep Blue. In 1997, this machine defeated reigning champion Garry Kasparov in a rematch, using 256 micro-processors that analyzed more than 100 million chess positions every single second. Some unusual chess terminology: a bad bishop (a bishop hemmed in by pawns of its own color), pins and skewers (forms of attack), and a zugzwang (when a player is disadvantaged by having to make a move).

On guard
Sir Prancealot of Wessex was getting anxious. Never the most courageous of knights, he'd called all his fellow men out on a full-scale alert (and on a Sunday lunchtime too) when he heard that Padrick of Cork and his ruffians were coming to invade.

Sir Prancealot's troops had gathered at the strategically important location of Puddleby-on-the-Marsh, which contains lots of arable land. His knights can occupy a square, and simultaneously protect up to eight squares as if they were a chess knight (see separate box on page 69).

A How many knights would Sir Prancealot need if each square in a 3 x 3 square area had to contain or be protected by at least one knight?

B How many knights would be needed to protect a 4 x 4 area?

C How can five knights protect a 5 x 5 area?

D What about eight knights protecting a 6 x 6 area?

E Place ten knights to guard a 7 x 7 area.

F Finally, suppose Sir Prancealot became paranoid and wanted to cover an 8 x 8 area with his men. Can it be done using just 12 knights? (Use the 8 x 8 chessboard on the opposite page if this helps.)

ANSWER page 94

Knight tracks

Sir Prancealot's troops waited, and waited…and waited some more. The enemy hadn't arrived, so they would have to go searching for them instead. Sir P. sent his chief knight on the lookout with two conditions. First, the knight had to walk directly from the center of one square to another, as if a chess knight were going "as the crow flies." Secondly, the conditions are so boggy that the knight must not cross his previous path lest the ground give way.

A Starting the knight from the center of any chosen square, verify that the knight can only make two trips on a 3 x 3 square field before he is forced to cross his previous path.

B What is the greatest number of trips the knight can make on a 4 x 4 board?

C Find a route that allows the knight to make ten trips on a 5 x 5 board.

D How can the knight make 16 trips on a 6 x 6 board?

E Discover a circular route of 24 consecutive jumps for a 7 x 7 board without crossing your tracks.

F What's the longest route you can find for an 8 x 8 board? A 35-move route is possible.

ANSWER page 95

Big knight out

What is the greatest number of knights that can be placed on a 7 x 7 chess board so that no two attack each other?

ANSWER page 95

Do you know...
How does a chess knight make its moves? It can move in up to eight different ways by moving two squares orthogonally immediately followed by a one-square sidestep, as shown here.

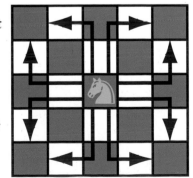

ON TOUR

"**A**ll aboard," shouted Tom Crook, travel agent to royalty, as the golden carriage rolled up to the palace steps. "I hope you're going to give us the grand tour," sniffed the queen, "since all my royal subjects deserve the chance to pay their respects to their ruler." "But only after we do a full security check first, ma'am," warned Major Rook. "No worries," comforted Tom, "and yes, Your Grace, we'll be visiting your dioceses too. Now let's get going, shall we?"

Did you know...
The classic design for modern chess sets is based on an 1835 design by the Englishman Nathaniel Cook. The patented design was endorsed by the world's best player at the time, Howard Staunton, and all international competitions today must be played using chess sets in the **Staunton pattern**.

The rook's tour

Before the queen visits all 64 areas of her domain, Major Rook demands that he do a full security check. Rook moves horizontally or vertically as far as he likes.

A How can Rook cover the entire board and return to his start position in just 16 moves? He can start wherever he likes, but must visit each square only once.

B How can Rook start at the top left corner, and enter every square of the board just once, finishing at the bottom right corner? It is possible once you know the trick!

ANSWER page 95

From A to B

Suppose a knight started at one corner of an 8 x 8 chessboard. Would it be possible for the knight to visit every other square and end up at the corner opposite the start position?

ANSWER page 95

The bishop's tour

Dr. White, the bishop, needed to visit his 32 dioceses by traveling through them all diagonally. As such, His Grace is confined to the squares of his color (besides, he wouldn't want to invade Reverend Black's patch). He may move as far as he wishes in a straight line at each move. How can Dr. White visit all 32 squares in 17 moves? The start and end points should be obvious, and squares can be revisited if necessary.

ANSWER page 95

The queen's tour

"This way, your majesty," said Tom Crook as he ushered the queen to the top left white corner square. "I'll wait here for you while you do your rounds." "Very well," sniffed the queen, "I shall return to this square once I've visited each of my 64 regions." The queen can move in a straight line in any of the eight directions. How can she tour the entire board in just 14 moves, ending back at the top left corner? Because no one will refuse the queen an audience, she can visit squares more than once

ANSWER page 95

The knight's tours

These beautiful drawings are formed by drawing the route taken by a knight doing a complete tour of the chessboard, then coloring the areas thus created.

The grand tour

The knight's tours illustrated in these diagrams involve the knight ending up at the square it started from. Is this possible on a 5 x 5 chessboard? 6 x 6? 7 x 7? Why?

ANSWER page 95

CHESSBOARD STANDOFF

"Get out of my way," snarled the Red Queen. "No, you get out of my way," snorted the White Queen. "And what on earth are all these other queens doing here?" The arrival of several of the most important chess pieces on the same board wasn't a particularly well-planned piece of diplomacy by the Master of the Board. Clearly, some clever positioning was going to be needed to keep the queens from attacking each other...

Chessboard standoff

On a 4 x 4 chessboard, only four queens can be placed so that no queen attacks another (see black squares on diagram).

A Place five queens on a 5 x 5 board so that no two lie in the same row, column, or any diagonal. (Use coins or counters on the board below to help you.)

B Now try six queens on a 6 x 6 board.

C How about seven queens on a 7 x 7 board?

D Finally, can you place eight queens on the large 8 x 8 board? Once you've found one solution, see if you can do it again so that there are no queens on the two main (longest) diagonals.

ANSWERS page 95

Chessboard jigsaw

Angered by her latest defeat, the Black Queen has banished the two white corners from the chessboard, leaving just 62 squares. Furthermore, she has ordered her pawns to cut up the remainder of the board into 31 individual 2 x 1 strips to ensure that no one can beat her again. Can the pawns accomplish this feat? If so, how? If not, why not?

ANSWER page 95

CHESSBOARD STANDOFF

A right royal mess

After a while, the queens were becoming more sociable. They were prepared to allow themselves to be under attack from exactly one other queen, so long as every queen agreed to this condition unanimously. You can see the result of this arrangement here—note how each and every queen is under attack from one, and only one, other queen.

A Suppose the queens relax further. How can the Master of the Board arrange 14 queens on the 8 x 8 board so that every queen is under attack from exactly two others?

B How can 16 queens be arranged so that every queen is under attack from exactly three others? (This is actually very easy.) Can you better 16 queens?

C For the grand finale, place 21 queens on the board so that every queen is attacked by exactly four others.

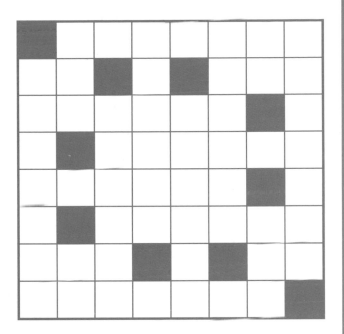

ANSWERS page 96

The world's best chess puzzle

If you know how to play chess, you'll appreciate this chess problem set by Sam Loyd, which takes some beating. In a chess problem, you are given a set-up board and an aim. In this case, the aim is to **play white and checkmate in five moves**, no matter what moves the black player chooses to make. We'll start you off: White (playing up the board) moves first and moves the **b2** pawn to **b4**. (Hint: This piece is very important.) Black is forced to move the rook at **c8** down to **c5** to stop the path of rook at **b5** (why?—because **b5** to **d5** to **d1** guarantees a checkmate within two more turns). Now complete the remaining four turns.

ANSWER page 96

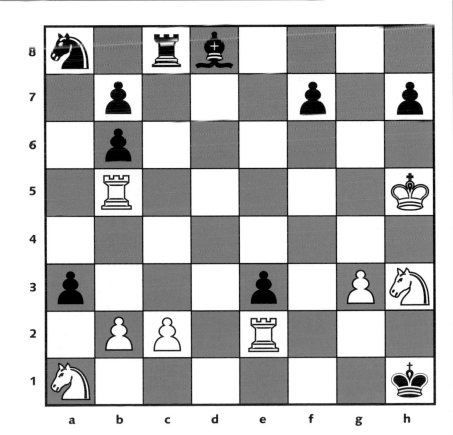

RIGHT THIS WAY

10

"**E**venin' sir, where to? Le Gavroche restaurant, no problem—on our way. Have you seen the roadworks around here lately? The number of diversions we've had this week is driving me round the twist. Just up here on the right. There you go, that'll be 14 royal portraits please. Oh, that's very kind of you, sir. By the way, you'll never guess who I had in the back of my cab last week..."

There or roundabouts

Here, our London cabbie has a complex roundabout to negotiate. Following the arrows at all times, how many different valid ways are there of going from A to B?

ANSWER page 96

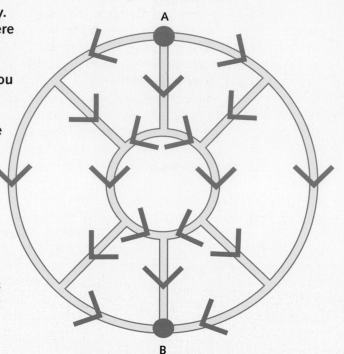

Congestion calamity

This time, the cab driver is trying to follow a complex set of one-way signs thanks to various roadworks currently in progress. Following the specified diversions at all times, how many different valid ways are there of getting from A to B? Can you find a logical method of solving these problems without having to count every single route?

ANSWER page 96

Hungry Horace

At the end of a hectic day, Horace the cab driver needs to drive straight home by the shortest route (i.e., south or east at all times). But because he is so hungry, he would like to visit a Sloppy Joe's Drive-Thru for some sustenance along the way. Luckily there are seven branches of Sloppy Joe's in the area. In order to avoid too much delay, he doesn't want to drive through two SJ's. So the puzzle is: How many ways are there of driving from his current position to home via the shortest route, going via **exactly one** branch of Sloppy Joe's?

ANSWER page 96

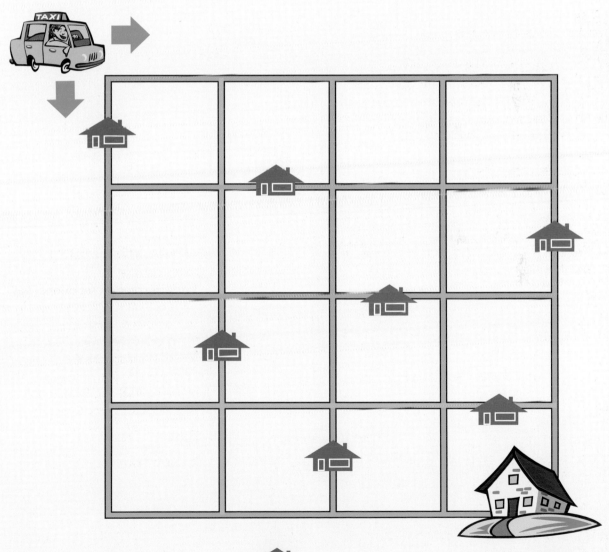

= Sloppy Joe's

home

TAXICAB GEOMETRY

"**H**ey buddy, welcome to New York. Where ya headin' to? Okay, Macy's it is. That's not too far—six blocks south and four blocks west. What's that, you say? Yeah, the city center is laid out in a grid system, saves people getting lost. There you go—that's 18 bucks please, buddy."

Fare's fair

Suppose you started your journey at point A and you wanted the New York cab driver to take you to point B by the shortest route possible. In other words, the taxi driver must always drive south or west from every junction.

A How many ways are there of the taxi taking you from A to B by the most economical route with a stopover at Central Park (point C)?

B How many ways are there of going from A to B by any shortest route?

HINT You can use a trick from the previous pages to work out this problem. Can you see a pattern in the numbers thus created?

ANSWER page 97

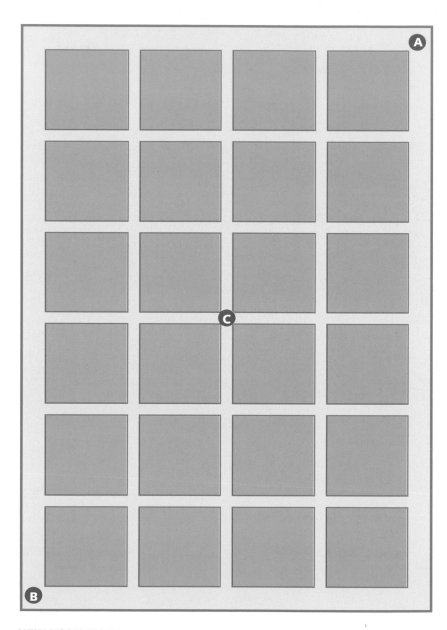

NEW YORK MAP
How many different routes are there from A to B by the shortest possible route?

Taxicab geometry

This grid represents a large-scale map of New York. Suppose a cab driver could follow only the lines (the "streets"). We call this "taxicab geometry," because it produces very different results from those you would normally expect, as these three exercises show:

A In normal (Euclidean) geometry, a circle is defined as a line connecting all the points that are a fixed distance from a given point. If our taxi driver began in the middle of the grid, what would a "circle" with a radius of three blocks (squares) look like? Try circles of other radii.

B On the grid, draw a "square" with four sides of six blocks in length. Remember always to draw along streets, never through the blocks. Are different solutions possible?

C In normal 2-D geometry, it would be impossible to draw a triangle with sides of 14, 8, and 6 units. (Why?) Try doing it in taxicab geometry.

ANSWER page 97

GRID FOR TAXICAB GEOMETRY

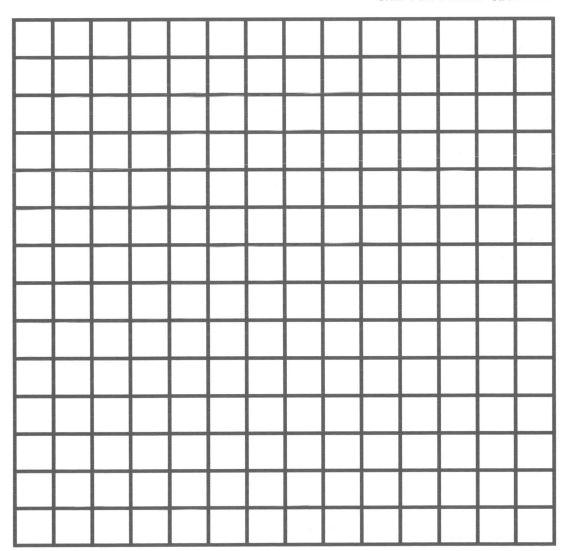

SPIDERWEBS

The ancient Greeks allowed only straight lines and circles in their geometry. But with a little imagination, even these simple elements can be used to create beautiful and unusual designs.

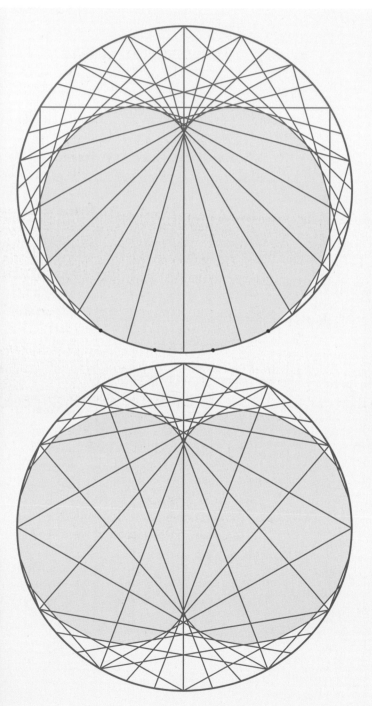

The circle line

Draw a circle, and divide its circumference into 36 equal parts at intervals of 10 degrees (use a protractor). Draw in a diameter of the circle— that is, a line joining one of these marked points to the point exactly opposite.

You are now going to draw a kind of spider's web, by moving this diameter. Move the top end one mark clockwise; but move the bottom end **two** marks clockwise. Join these marks. Now repeat, and continue until you get back to where you started from, always moving one end one mark and the other end two marks. You will find that you have created a heart-shaped curve called a **cardioid** (above left).

Now that you've got the hang of this, what happens if you move the top end of the diameter by one mark (as before), but you move the bottom end by three marks? You obtain a kidney-shaped curve called a **nephroid** (below left).

Try these on your own:

A Move the top end of the diameter by two marks and the bottom end by three. You should obtain a buttercup curve (**ranunculoid**).
B Move the top end of the diameter by one mark and the bottom end by four marks.
C Move the top end of the diameter by two marks and the bottom end by five marks.

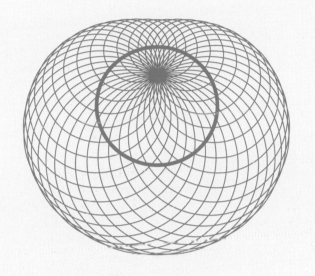

The drunken spider

If the spider is drunk, it will weave its web in circles instead of straight lines. This leads to new possibilities for designs. As before, draw a **base circle** (the thick black line) and mark it into 36 equal segments, 10 degrees per segment. Also, mark a **home point** somewhere on the diagram.

Now take a pair of compasses and place the needle on one of the points on the base circle, and open the compasses so that the pencil lead just touches the home point. Draw this circle. Remove the compasses, and repeat with all the other points on the base circle. Note how every circle will have its center on the base circle and includes the home point somewhere on its circumference.

When you've finished, you'll have created a **limaçon** (above left). Changing the location of the home point gives different shapes, as you can see (left).

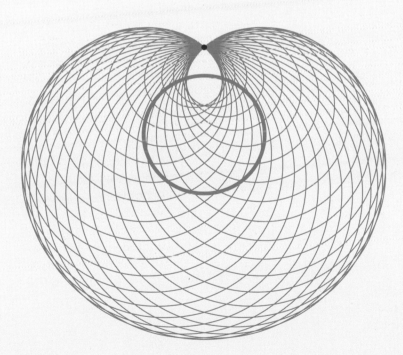

OPEN EXERCISE

Try a home point that lies on the base circle. Do you recognize the curve?

HAVE YOUR CAKE AND...

11

MAP MADNESS

Cath's Crazy Cakes has been providing after-dinner confectionery to the good people of Greenchester for over ten years. Cath is well known for her use of unusual eye-catching Art Deco–style designs. Never have lines and circles been so tasty. Unfortunately, Cath's fridge is getting on in years and today's the day it's finally going to snap...

Cake calamity

The thermostat in Cath's fridge had given up the ghost. So, when she came in one Monday she found that her beautiful square, decorated cakes had become somewhat misshapen. In particular, the frosting had melted badly. For each of the three cakes pictured, can you say which one had the original square design shown above it?

ANSWER page 97

A

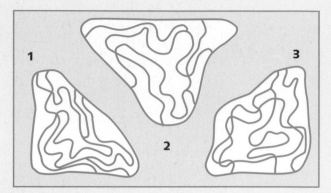

1   3

2

B

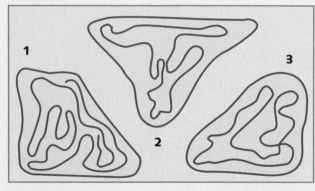

1   3

2

C

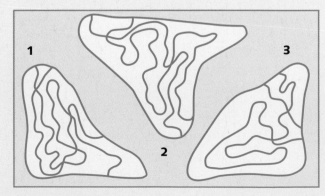

1   3

2

?

Did you know...

There is a whole branch of mathematics that examines knots. **Knot theory** is a branch of topology that has many unsolved problems. A knot may be thought of as a loop of rubber that can be twisted, stetched, or otherwise deformed in ordinary three-dimensional space, but not torn. Two knots are said to be equivalent if one can be deformed into the other. A complete set of characteristics that is sufficient to distinguish all knots has not been devised. However, the science has many practical applications, including the study of complex chemical molecules such as DNA.

Dough handcuffs

Cath was playing with some stretchy bread dough in her shop. She first made a design such as the one shown near right, which resemble some linked handcuffs. She then played around with the dough, deforming it but without making or filling in any holes. She found, to her surprise, that she could unlink the cuffs just by deforming the dough. See if you can do the same, either with some modeling clay or just using your mind's eye.

ANSWER page 97

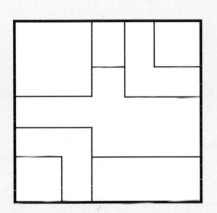
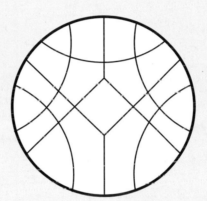
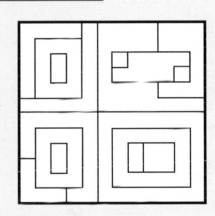

Frosting on the cake

Cath always knew that she needed at most four colors of frosting to complete any of the geometric designs on her cakes. Above are three cakes that have been designed but haven't yet been frosted. Cath frosts her cakes so that no two areas sharing a border have the same color. Can you work out the smallest number of colors of frosting needed to cover each of these cakes completely?

ANSWER page 98

?

Did you know...

To a topologist, a donut and a teacup with a handle are essentially the same thing because they both have one hole. If you make a teacup out of rubber or modeling clay, you can gradually transform it into a donut without sealing or creating any holes—this is why topology is sometimes called "rubber sheet" geometry. Note that for something to be a hole, you must be able to thread right through it. The bit where the tea goes is therefore not a hole.

PAINTING BY NUMBERS

Charlie Satchel is an esteemed collector of new wave British modern art, and a particular fan of the Mondrian style. It was with some delight, therefore, that he discovered a young artist named Hamish Durst working in the backwaters of Islington in London. Durst's latest four paintings are stark and geometrical, but Satchel insisted that he color them because they would be more valuable that way. But is it art?

Modern art

Durst got out his paintbox to start the process of coloring in his black and white paintings. But how many colors would he need?

A For each of the paintings shown, what is the **least** number of colors required to cover each canvas such that no two adjacent areas have the same color?

B Can you **prove** your answer? In other words, can you provide a logical, reasoned argument as to why your answer is correct?

ANSWER page 98

Brams' map-coloring game

This more advanced map-coloring game is named for its inventor, Steven Brams.

Set-up

Using a black pen, draw any map you like, such as the example given here. You will also need five or six colored pens or pencils.

How to play

Players take turns to color any blank area of the map, always obeying the rule that areas with a common border must not be the same color.

Aim

PLAYER 1 is the **minimizer**. This player's aim is to ensure that the entire map has been colored with five or fewer colors.

PLAYER 2 is the **maximizer**. This player's aim is to use as many different colors as possible. However, if a valid move is possible, this player is forced to make it.

Winning

If the maximizer **cannot** play a valid move using any of the five pens, the maximizer wins. If the entire diagram is completed correctly (no two adjacent areas are the same color), the minimizer wins.

Advanced version

Once you've got the hang of the game, try a more complicated map with more areas and use six colored pens instead of five.

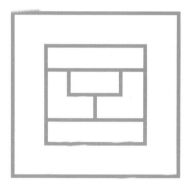

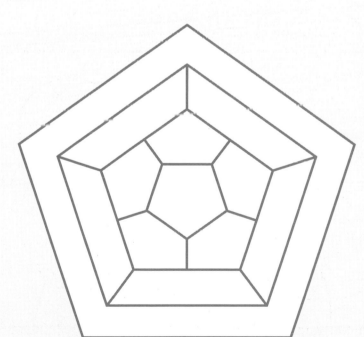

Winning Brams' game

Suppose you were playing the Brams' game on this pentagonal map with five colored pens. How could you force a win playing as the maximizer? In other words, what tactic could you employ to ensure that, no matter what moves the minimizer made, you would win?

HINT The third dimension is useful.

ANSWER page 98

COLORING THE COLONY

Sir Frederick Featherstonehaugh and Lord Bertram of Buckley were arguing over the course of history. "Had Mafeking gone the other way, you see, it could have all been so much different," claimed Sir Frederick.

"Nonsense," retorted Lord Bertram. "The 14th Fusiliers would have seen us through." Both gentlemen reached for their napkins and started jotting down their plans for world domination.

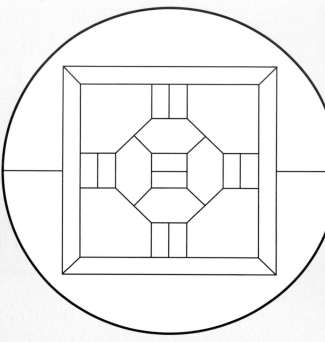

World domination—Part 1

Sir Frederick drew the diagram on the left to demonstrate the rigid structure in which the northern hemisphere should have been divided up. "To prevent any one empire getting too much power," said Sir F. as he twitched his mustache as if to signal a masterstroke, "we'd separate them into two different areas."

How could Sir Frederick colonize his map using 12 colors (each one used in exactly two areas) so that no two adjacent empires are the same color? The catch is that each color is treated as the same empire: So, for example, if the first area of your yellow empire borders red and dark green, the **other** yellow empire (which is elsewhere on the map) must not border a red or dark green area either.

ANSWER page 98

World domination—Part 2

Lord Bertram quietly choked at Sir Frederick's insolence. "I rather think, dear chap, that the world will be somewhat more organic. And moreover, the growth of travel will mean that the communities will be much more widespread."

How can Lord Bertram use 18 colors (or, if you prefer, numbers) so that no two adjacent empires are the same color? This time each color (or number) must have **three** separate areas that are all treated as the same empire: So, for example, if your first two yellow areas collectively touch red, pale green, dark blue, and black, the **third** area of the yellow empire cannot border those colors. We have started you off—you have eight colors (numbers 1 to 8) to complete.

ANSWER page 98

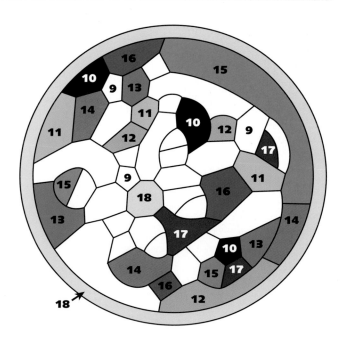

Galactic domination

After rather too many glasses of Port, Lord Bertram and Sir Frederick were now fighting over how Mars should be colonized in the future. "The way I see it," snorted the lord, "is that if a group has two separate settlements on Earth, they should also be separate on Mars." The knight nodded sagely in agreement.

Regions with the same number must be colored the same on Earth and on Mars. So, for example, if you choose yellow for 1, both the 1 areas must be yellow. You may use a color for more than one number, but at no time may any two areas of the same color share a border on either planet.

For example, while areas 2 and 8 are not adjacent on the map of Earth, they cannot be given the same color because they are adjacent on Mars. The challenge is to color both maps entirely using the fewest possible colors.

HINT The answer is at least eight.

ANSWER page 98

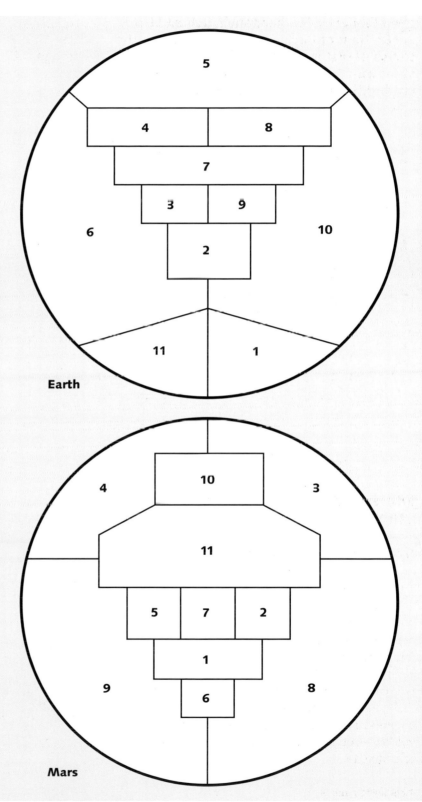

GET LOST

12

MAZES

One of the most famous maze legends concerns the paradigmatic Labyrinth of King Minos of Crete, built by Daedalus to house the Minotaur. Theseus found his way out by using a ball of golden thread. It is doubtful that this maze, said to have been situated near Knossos, ever existed, although it was represented on coins. However, other real mazes have existed for more than 4,000 years.

Maze connections

Amazingly (sorry!), all early labyrinths consisted of just one winding path. They were used as a recreational or spiritual path along which you could walk while meditating, for instance. It is only in the past few centuries that the concept of a puzzle maze, with a choice of routes, has emerged.

From the mathematical standpoint, there are only two categories of puzzle maze. The next time you are in a life-size maze, try this experiment. Place your hand on the left-hand (or right-hand) wall and keep walking forward. No matter what happens, keep walking without letting go of the wall, and let your hand guide you. The chances are that this method will usually get you to the middle but not necessarily by the shortest route. This type of maze is described as **simply connected**, because all the walls are connected to one another.

If the maze designer is particularly sneaky, he will use a **multiply connected** design. Here, the "hand on the wall" technique doesn't work because some of the walls are effectively free-standing—that is, not connected to the outer walls. Try using the hand on the wall method on these two mazes.

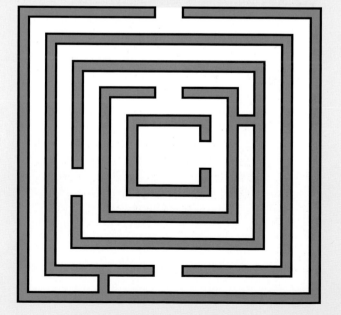

TWO TYPES OF MAZE
Top: a simply connected maze
Right: a multiply connected maze

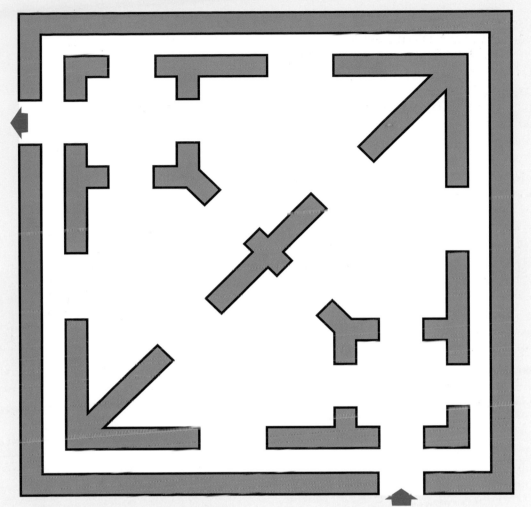

MAZE PROBLEM
*Help Theseus
to escape one
more time.*

? Who was...Daedalus?
He was a mythical Greek architect
who was said to have built many
structures, including King Minos's
labyrinth. After an argument,
Daedalus was imprisoned by Minos,
so to escape he made wings of wax
and feathers for himself and Icarus,
his son. Unfortunately, Icarus flew
too near the sun, his wings melted,
and he drowned in the sea.

Door to door
Can you help Theseus escape through this
maze? The catch is that he must run through
every door once, and never retrace any part of
his route.

ANSWER page 98

ANSWERS

ANSWERS

The impossible domino bridge problem PAGE 5

Use two extra dominoes as supports (as shown) then pull them away once the structure has been built.

The horse-and-rider problem PAGE 5

The trick is to place the riders so that one horse's head matches up with the other horse's rear!

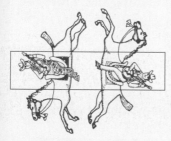

The circles-coloring problem PAGE 6

The color of each circle depends on the number of other circles it is touching.

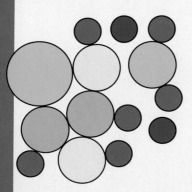

The classic T-puzzle PAGE 6

This is how the pieces fit together correctly.

The square game PAGE 6

In this exercise you were invited to draw a square. Typically, when invited to do such a simple task, we think of doing the "usual" thing, that is:

Take the pen that I've been given and put it in my hand (usually my right hand) and draw a square (a four-sided geometric object) on the only piece of paper that was available to me.

Creativity and lateral thinking are all about breaking these conventions. When first presented with this exercise, most people draw about eight squares of varying sizes and maybe a couple more squares on the diagonal. But there are plenty more ways of achieving the set task than that. If alternative solutions don't come naturally out of thin air, you can still be creative by analyzing the process logically, breaking down the steps then thinking of ways of performing each step differently:

■ I need to draw something. I have a pen, but **what other pens could I use**? Where could I obtain these from? Could I draw something without a pen? What about using lipstick?

■ Instead of putting the pen into my hand, **what other parts of my body or tools could I use**?

■ Is there something I could **change about the way I draw**? Could I make a square smaller, or larger, or draw it at an angle? Could I use dotted lines, press the pen down harder, or draw in perspective?

■ When I think of the word "square," I normally think of a four-sided geometric object. **What other definitions are there of the word "square?"** e.g., square number, Times square, an unfashionable person, the words "A SQUARE."

■ I need to draw something but **not necessarily on the piece of paper**. Could I draw on someone else's paper? Could I use a flipchart? Draw it on my hand (I can always wash it off)? On someone else's shirt (I can always buy them a nicer one)? Draw it on a steamed-up window? Draw an imaginary square in the air?

■ **Am I really on my own here?** No one actually said that I couldn't ask other people for suggestions.

From X to Y PAGE 7

Replace X and Y with (°)C and (°)F respectively. In Celsius and Fahrenheit temperature terms, 10°C = 50°F and so on.

Speed demon PAGE 7

By sneezing!

Cheating the heating PAGE 7

Turning down the radiators in the room that contains the central heating thermostat will make the heating turn on sooner, so the rest of the house will become warmer.

Get the point? PAGE 7

Ten, including the white arrow that can be seen pointing in the opposite direction from all the others.

Animal magic PAGE 7

Elephant (some of the letters have to be turned upside-down).

Very handy PAGE 7

Two—if one is the wrong kind of handedness, simply turn that rubber glove inside-out.

Rural areas PAGE 10

A The farmer can form 11 regions using 4 fences.

B 16 regions are possible with 5 fences.

C Writing out the results so far as a number series, we get: 1, 2, 4, 7, 11, 16. In other words, we add one, then add two, then add three … and so on.

D The key to finding a formula for this series is the pattern 0x1, 1x2, 2x3, 3x4, 4x5, 5x6 etc. This gives us 0, 2, 6, 12, 20, 30… which, if we halve the results, is already very close: 0, 1, 3, 6, 10, 15… If we just add one to every term, we obtain our desired series. What we have done is take a number, multiply it by the next largest whole number, divide the result by two then add one. Therefore, if Farmer Giles has **n** fences available, the number of crops he can grow is given by the formula (**n** x (**n** +1))/2 + 1.

This problem is one of the simplest in a branch of mathematics known as **combinatorial geometry**. There is a fascinating interplay between shapes and numbers. A great many variations on the theme are possible.

De-fence-less PAGE 11

Farmer Gill's three sizes of triangles are shown below.

This arrangement, a little like the Star of David on the Israeli flag, does the trick.

Pizza palaver PAGE 11

Cut the pizza into quarters, then stack the quarters into a pile. The final cut through the stack creates the eight identical pieces required.

Cutting the cake PAGE 11

Your first cut would cut the cake into two pieces. Your second straight cut, at best, can cut these into a total of four pieces. Likewise, your third straight cut creates eight pieces. It doesn't matter how you rearrange the cake—a straight knife can cut a straight-edged piece of cake into only two pieces at best.

Weld done PAGE 12

Each new strip of lead line adds one more weld (intersection) than the last piece of lead added. In table form:

LINES	INTERSECTIONS	TOTAL
2	1	1
3	1 + 2	3
4	1 + 2 + 3	6
5	1 + 2 + 3 + 4	10
6	1 + 2 + 3 + 4 + 5	15
7	1 + 2 + 3 + 4 + 5 + 6	21

Why does this work? For each new line added, all that is necessary is for it to avoid passing through the previous intersections, and to avoid being parallel to any of the previous lines. Despite these conditions, this means that out of the infinite number of possible lines we could add, there are still many that could work. Hence, it is indeed possible to make each line meet all the others. So, when we add the fifth line, there is no reason why it can't cross all of the previous four, and so on for any number you choose.

The series 1, 3, 6, 10, 15, 21…is known as **triangular numbers**. Can you see why? If not, get some coins or counters of the same size and try arranging them. The formula that generates the number of welds for **n** strips is ½**n**(**n** − 1).

Art deco-ration PAGE 13

Any valid solution would do fine, although the solution illustrated boasts an impressive 11 triangles.

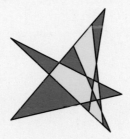

Gone to pot PAGE 13

There are three other possible arrangements, as shown here.

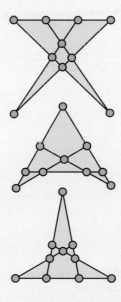

Did you know?

Where did the ½**n**(**n** − 1) formula come from? Let's call the triangle number formed from **n** lines T(**n**). When we had five lines, we added together 1 + 2 + 3 + 4. Therefore, by definition, T(**n**) = 1 + 2 + 3 +…+ (**n** − 2) + (**n** − 1). Writing that backwards (no reason we can't), T(**n**) = (**n** − 1) + (**n** − 2) +…+ 3 + 2 + 1. Adding those two equations together gives us: 2 T(**n**) = **n** + **n** +…+ **n** + **n**. That's 2 T(**n**) = **n** − 1 lots of **n**, or **n** × (**n** − 1). Dividing both sides of the equation by 2 gives us T(**n**) = ½**n**(**n** − 1).

Nine areas PAGE 14

The key to this is to do what management consultants say they do: think outside the box. If you didn't see how to solve it, you've run head first into a conceptual block, and a typical one: the tendency to take too narrow a view of the problem. Are you assuming that the lines must be horizontal or vertical? Certainly, that's how the dots naturally arrange themselves…but nobody said the lines had to go in any particular direction. Diagonals would provide new possibilities.

Then again, although the square of dots has a natural square boundary, nothing in the problem says that your lines have to stay **within** that boundary. Mental walls…

The great value of an insight is that, once gained, it may be applied, as a general rule, to other similar problems. The solution is shown below as a solid line.

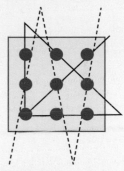

Sneaky solution PAGE 14

The method is shown as a dotted line on the **Nine areas** solution above.

Twelve areas PAGE 15

Two different types of diagonal line are needed for this one. Five lines are needed in total.

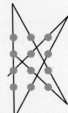

Sixteen areas PAGE 15

Two different types of diagonal line are also needed for this solution.

ANSWERS

Bridge the gaps PAGE 16

No, it is not possible to cross all seven bridges only once each. Euler solved this problem by replacing the real map with a topological equivalent. He then postulated that you could complete the journey only if there were either 0 or 2 places where an odd number of routes meet. Since the Königsberg bridges area has **four** junctions with an odd number of lines, no solution can exist.

At a stroke PAGE 17

For the general rule, consider this: There are essentially two different types of journey: **(a)** ones we start and end at the same place, and **(b)** ones we end at a different place from where we started. In case **(a)**, every junction must have an even number of "roads." This is because for every junction we enter, we have to be able to get out again so that we can get back to our starting point. In case **(b)**, we need even numbers of roads at every intersection **except** for the start and finish points, which must have odd numbers of roads. This is because we don't want to return to the start point.

So the general rule is: **If a connected map has 0 or 2 junctions where an odd number of roads meet, it can be traversed.** If there are 0 odd junctions, you can start anywhere. If there are 2 odd junctions, those are your start and finish points. Using this knowledge, it's easy to see that the hot cross bun and diamond pattern (diagrams 1 and 4) can't be traversed as they both have 4 odd junctions. The envelope with flap (diagram 2) is possible as long as you start and finish using the bottom corners because these are the two odd junctions. It is possible to complete the five-pointed star (diagram 3) from anywhere.

Not impossible after all PAGE 17

Fold the page of the book and use the other side of the paper to get you out of sticky situations! Repeat as necessary until the diagram is complete.

Child's play PAGE 19

1 Scalene triangle—1 way
2 Isosceles triangle—2 ways
3 Parallelogram (slanted rectangle)—2 ways
4 Rhombus (slanted square)—4 ways
5 Equilateral triangle—6 ways
6 Square—8 ways
7 Cross—8 ways
8 Tetrahedron (pyramid)—12 ways
9 Cube—24 ways

Missing length PAGE 19

An isosceles triangle has two sides of equal length (by definition) so the third side must be 4 or 9 units long. But it can't be 4 units long, because you can't form a triangle with sides of 4, 4, and 9 units length (can you see why?) So the third side must be 9 units long.

A new angle PAGE 19

By drawing the triangle on a sphere. Suppose the Earth was perfectly round. If you drew a line from the North Pole to the equator, then a quarter of the way around the equator, then back to the North Pole, the line would have turned 90 degrees at each stage. Therefore the total of all three angles is 270 degrees. This is called a **trirectangular** triangle. A triangle's angles total 180 degrees only when it is on a flat plane.

100% proof PAGE 20

Cutting the smallest square into pieces allows us to reassemble it with the middle-sized shape to form the larger square. Since the square whose side is the hypotenuse has exactly the same area as the two other squares combined, we have proved the theorem.

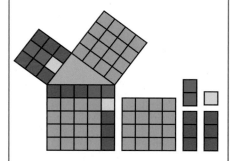

Third base PAGE 20

If the two shorter sides of the triangle are 8 and 17 units long, then $8^2 + 17^2 = x^2$, where **x** is the number we seek. However, $8^2 + 17^2 = 353$, and 353 doesn't have a square root that is a whole number. Therefore, 17 must be the length of the hypotenuse. In this case, $x^2 + 8^2 = 17^2 = 289$. Putting this another way, $x^2 = 289 - 64 = 225$. The square root of 225 is 15 (since 15 x 15 = 225), so the third side is 15 units long.

Pythagorean puzzle PAGE 21

Here's how to arrange the pieces:

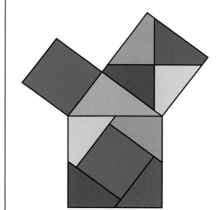

Deluxe jewelry PAGE 22

The number of wires is 1, 3, 6, 10, 15...so we add + 1, + 2, + 3, + 4, + 5...each time. Therefore the series will continue 21, 28, 36...and so on. These are the **triangular numbers**, which we met in the answer to page 12.

Runes PAGE 22

There are 12 possibilities with five clasps and 60 possible designs with six clasps. Suppose we numbered the clasps from 1 to 6. If Janice draws the black line design around clasps 1, 3, 4, 6, 5, 2 (and back to 1) this is the same as the design 6, 5, 2, 1, 3, 4 (and back to 6) because they are the same loop, just starting at a different point. So we need concern ourselves only with five points of the route and can assume that all the loops start from the same point. At first there are five points to choose from, then four, then three, etc., so there are 5 x 4 x 3 x 2 x 1 = 120 possibilities for six clasps. But, because each design also looks the same when drawn backward, we need to halve this result, which is where the answer 60 comes from. For **n** clasps, the general formula is all the numbers from 1 to (**n** – 1) multiplied together then divided by 2. Mathematicians write this as (**n** – 1)!/2. The **factorial** symbol ! represents the product of all the numbers.

Galaxy game PAGE 23

One possible route is shown here:

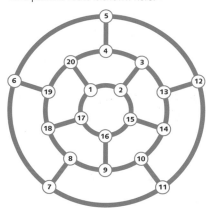

The inventor of this puzzle, Sir William Rowan Hamilton, was born in Dublin in 1805 and by the age of nine could speak 13 different languages. He is best known in the fields of mathematics and astronomy. In 1828, he was made Astronomer Royal for Ireland. In the field of dynamics he introduced **Hamiltonian functions**, which express the sum of the kinetic and potential energies of a moving object. They were important in the development of modern-day **quantum mechanics**. He originally sold the idea of his Hamilton game for £25 (about $38, which was about what $835 is worth today) in 1859.

The utilities problem PAGE 24

It you try drawing a line from each house to each utility, you find that eight lines are possible but the final ninth line is somewhat trickier. Therefore, the problem seems impossible. In mathematical terms, it is indeed impossible to connect three nodes to three nodes in every way possible without the lines crossing. However, it is **practically** possible if one of the home owners permits one wire or pipe to run under his house!

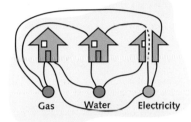

Off to work we go PAGE 25

It is possible, as shown here:

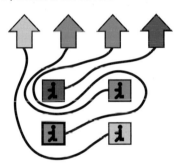

Upsizing PAGE 25

Yes. In fact, any number of workers can be connected to the same number of offices without their paths crossing. Try it and see for yourself.

Ground plan PAGE 26

With three towns, there are three ways—each town takes a turn to be the town in the middle of the other two. As we know, there are 16 ways for four towns. Noting the clue about this being a "powerful" series, perhaps the pattern goes:

3 to the power of 1 = 3

4 to the power of 2 = 4 x 4 = 16

5 to the power of 3 = 5 x 5 x 5 = 125

6 to the power of 4 = 6 x 6 x 6 x 6 = 1296

and so on.

This is indeed the correct answer, so Fifetons will have to consider 125 different road layouts. The general formula is: **n** to the power of **n** – 2. This even works for **n** = 2, because 2 to the power of 0 is 1 (by definition) and there is just one way of connecting two towns together.

Lang time, no see PAGE 26

The best solution is to make the junctions join at 120 degrees, as shown here.

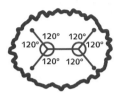

Tangram challenges PAGE 33

Double tangram puzzle PAGE 34

The two simplest solutions retain the pieces in their original configuration because they form two more large triangles that complete the square.

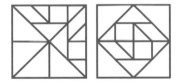

Five-piece suite PAGE 37

Here's how to create each shape.

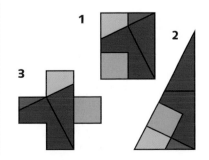

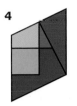
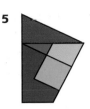

Squarea PAGE 37

If you refer back to the illustration in the original **Five-piece suite** puzzle, you will see that the central square is surrounded by four triangles and four quadrilaterals. It is not difficult to see that, with a little rearrangement, each triangle and quadrilateral can be made to form a square of the same size as the central one. In other words, the 100 square units of area can be divided up into five identical squares. Therefore, each piece is 20 square units—and that's the answer.

Number jig PAGE 37

The answer to both questions is 999. This is because each jigsaw piece needs to be connected to one other piece or group of pieces at some point.

Hexagon to triangle puzzle PAGE 38

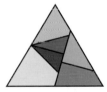

Six-pointed star puzzle PAGE 38

Stars puzzle PAGE 39

The configuration of each star (using different colors) is:

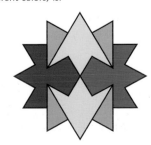

ANSWERS

Boxing clever PAGE 41

This is the best solution to date. These problems are fiendishly difficult to prove outright, and until someone comes up with a proof, there's always a possibility that someone can come up with a better solution.

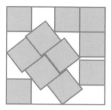

Patio ratio PAGE 42

The solutions for even-numbered squares (2 x 2, 4 x 4, 6 x 6 etc.) should be obvious—it's just four squares of the same size taking up one quarter of the area of each.

The solutions for the other, odd-numbered sizes are as follows:

3x3

5x5

7x7

9x9

11x11

13x13

Separate the sisters PAGE 44

With a bit of luck these designs will earn Mr. Moore some peace and quiet.

Sequestrate the siblings PAGE 45

Each room can be divided into four as follows:

Ernie's enigma PAGE 48

Here are the completed diagrams. There may be other solutions for any particular case. Now try making up your own puzzles—there are around 50 known ways of placing the tiles together so that all edges match.

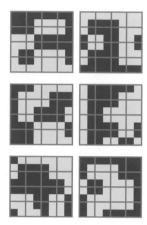

Open exercise PAGE 49

Eight moves is the fewest possible. In the diagram below, none of the leftover pieces could be played in one of the eight remaining spaces without breaking the rules of the game.

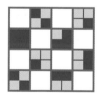

Hexabits puzzle PAGE 51

This is one possible answer.

Domino derby PAGE 52

Other solutions are possible.

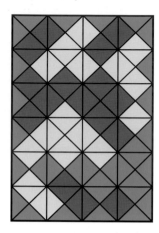

Domino rally PAGE 53

Other solutions are possible.

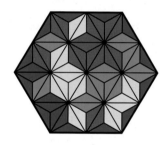

How many bones? PAGE 53

There are seven different symbols (blank, 1, 2, 3, 4, 5, 6) that have to appear eight times (twice on a symbol's double, and once on the other six pieces). 7 x 8 = 56. Each piece can display two different symbols, so 56/2 = 28. So there are 28 pieces in a standard set.

The Lo-shu magic square PAGE 54

All rows, columns, and both diagonals add up to the magic number 15.

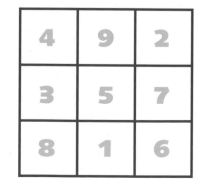

4	9	2
3	5	7
8	1	6

A diabolic square PAGE 54

This is called a diabolic magic square because there are a diabolical number of ways of getting the magic number (34). For example, the numbers in each quarter of the large square total 34. The middle 2x2 square totals 34. Some broken diagonals such as 2-8-9-15 total 34. How many others can you find? Incidentally, the 15 and 14 in the bottom row denote the year that Dürer created his etching.

16	3	2	13
5	10	11	8
9	6	7	12
4	15	14	1

Latin square of order 5 PAGE 55

One way is shown below (It should be noted that Euler's Latin squares were not concerned with long diagonals. However, the squares were the basis of an important area of mathematics called group theory.)

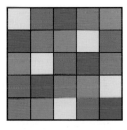

Latin square of order 6 PAGE 55

36 tiles are impossible. A solution for 32 tiles is:

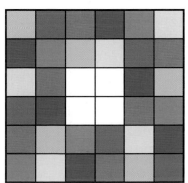

Can you find a better solution?

The tricky eight PAGE 56

The trick is to use fractions, as shown. Note that the middle box must always be one-third of the magic number, making the middle 8-5-2 column easy to establish.

4½	8	2½
3	5	7
7½	2	5½

In the red PAGE 56

The magic number is always three times the central number (for 3x3 magic squares). Here the middle number is 3, so the magic number must be 9. From here, it is easy to work out the rest of the grid and deduce that negative numbers are required:

6	-1	4
1	3	5
2	7	0

Versatile squares PAGE 57

A

2	1	4
3	5	7
6	9	8

B

12	1	18
9	6	4
2	36	3

C

3	1	2
9	6	4
18	36	12

Devilish dozen PAGE 57

This is one of several possible solutions.

	1	10	
3	5	8	12
7	11	2	4
	9	6	

That's odd PAGE 57

Note how the odd numbers have a very simple arrangement, as if in diagonal rows of different lengths:

14	10	1	22	18
20	11	7	3	24
21	17	13	9	5
2	23	19	15	6
8	4	25	16	12

Postman's knock PAGE 59

Given that "the number of houses does not matter," you can assume there are two houses. The postman will either get both letters into the correct letterboxes or they will be swapped around, so the average number of correct deliveries is (2 + 0)/2 = 1. In fact, the average result is always 1 even if you have 100 houses and 100 letters.

What are the odds? PAGE 59

A There are 5 x 4 x 3 x 2 x 1 ways of addressing the cards, but only one way is completely correct. Hence, the probability is 1/120.

B Zero, because if one envelope is wrong then at least one other envelope must be wrong also.

Window shield PAGE 60

Here's one possible design for Bob's window.

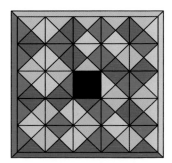

ANSWERS

Hexagons or cubes PAGE 62

Here's one possible solution. Put together in this way the hexagons resemble cubes.

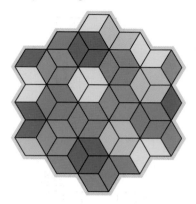

Dance floor dominoes PAGE 64

Note that where four tiles touch corners, there is a high degree of symmetry (by necessity).

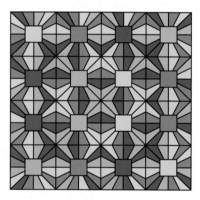

DJ display PAGE 65

A green zigzag cannot be made.

Drive time PAGE 65

It is a certainty. To see why, imagine that Groovy Stu is driving his car and that his twin brother Mike Fab is driving the cab at the same times, but instead they choose to drive **on the same day**. Stu and Mike must pass each other at some point.

Sixth form PAGE 66

Thirteen designs are possible, as shown here.

For 6 yellows: There is only one possibility (all the same)

For 5 yellow, 1 red: There is only one possibility, since the red bead can be rotated to anywhere on the necklace.

For 4 yellow, 2 red: The two red beads can either be next to each other, one bead apart, or two beads apart (i.e., opposite each other). This gives three unique possibilities.

For 3 yellow, 3 red: There is one way the reds can be all bunched up, one way the reds can be separate, and one unique way to have 2 reds + 1 red elsewhere. This is three in total.

So far, that is 1 + 1 + 3 + 3 = 8. However, we can cut down the work for the remaining three cases because they are the same as the first three but with the colors reversed. So the total is 2 x (1 + 1 + 3) + 3 = 13.

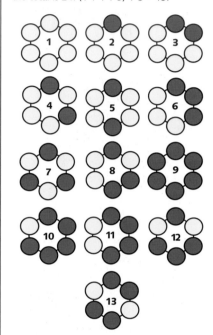

Guess what? PAGE 66

There are 27,012 different ways of making a 20-bead necklace using two colors of beads. How close did you get?

Seventh heaven PAGE 67

Using a similar analysis to the previous puzzle:

For 7 yellows: There is only one possibility (all the same).

For 6 yellow, 1 red: There is only one possibility, since the red segment can be rotated to anywhere on the brooch.

For 5 yellow, 2 red: The two red triangles can either be next to each other, one section apart, or two sections apart. This gives three unique possibilities.

For 4 yellow, 3 red: There is one way the reds can be all bunched up, one way the reds

can be separate, and two unique ways with 2 reds + 1 red elsewhere. This is four in total.

This totals 1 + 1 + 3 + 4 = 9 ways so far. All the other cases are the same as these with the colors reversed, so there must be 18 in total, as shown here.

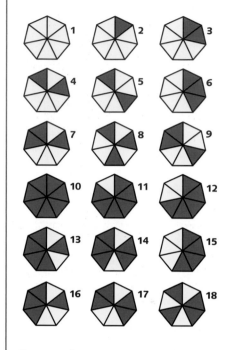

On guard PAGE 68

Each of the squares in these 3 x 3 to 8 x 8 grids either contains a knight or is attacked by one.

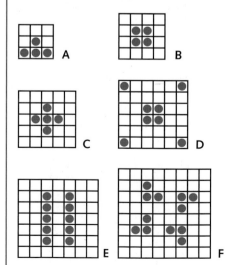

Knight tracks PAGE 69

The best solutions for 3 x 3 to 8 x 8 grids are given here.

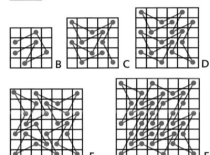

Big knight out PAGE 69

Note that a knight always attacks squares that are different from the color of square it is currently on. A 7 x 7 chessboard has 25 black squares and 24 white squares. By placing one knight on every black square, only white squares will be attacked. Therefore, 25 is the correct answer.

The rook's tour PAGE 70

A This is one solution. (It is surprising how many 17-move solutions there are, and how difficult it is to find a 16-move solution like this.)

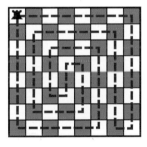

B The catch in the question was that Rook had to **enter** every square just once—i.e., he could revisit the start point. This makes the problem possible:

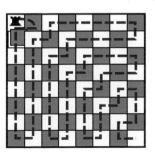

From A to B PAGE 70

No, because the knight will make 63 jumps (an odd number), so will finish on a different color square from the one on which he started. Opposite squares of an 8 x 8 chessboard are the same color.

The bishop's tour PAGE 71

Here is one way His Grace can do the rounds. Note that he has to start in one white corner and finish in the other.

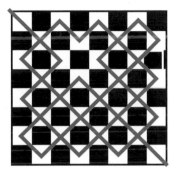

The queen's tour PAGE 71

Here's one way to conduct the royal visit.

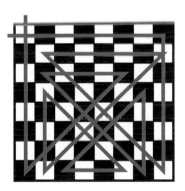

The grand tour PAGE 71

It is not possible on any square chessboard with an odd number of squares (such as 5 x 5 or 7 x 7). For example, on a 5 x 5 chessboard, the knight will make 24 jumps before returning home. The knight will end the 24th jump on a square of the same color to the start position. The final leap back home is therefore impossible, because a knight cannot jump from a black square to a black square (the same is true for white to white). It is possible on a 6x6 chessboard.

Chessboard standoff PAGE 72

A 2 ways. The second is the mirror image of this one.

B 1 way

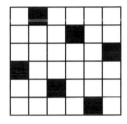

C 6 ways. This is one of them.

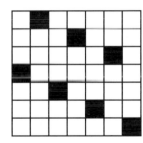

D There are 12 unique solutions for placing eight queens on an 8 x 8 grid, only two of which don't use the main diagonals. This is one of them.

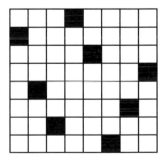

Chessboard jigsaw PAGE 72

It's not possible, because removing two opposite corners of the chessboard removes two squares of the same color. Since each 2 x 1 piece contains a square of either color, you will always be left with two individual squares of the same color.

ANSWERS

A right royal mess PAGE 73

A

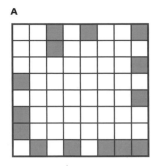

B

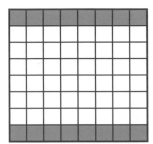

B (ii) This solution uses 18 queens.

C

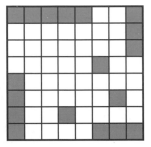

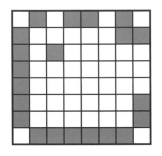

The world's best chess puzzle PAGE 73

The full solution, complete with black's best possible replies, is:

MOVE 1: WHITE: Pawn **b2** to **b4**
BLACK: Rook **c8** to **c5** (white in check)

MOVE 2: WHITE: Pawn **b4** takes **c5**
BLACK: Pawn **a3** to **a2**

MOVE 3: WHITE: Pawn **c5** to **c6**
BLACK: Bishop **d8** to **c7**

MOVE 4: WHITE: Pawn **c6** takes **b7**
BLACK: (doesn't matter)

MOVE 5: WHITE: Pawn **b7** takes **a8**, and upgrades to a queen.

This checkmates the black king, because he cannot escape to **g1** (protected by knight at **h3**) nor **g2** and **h2** (protected by rook at **e2**).

Note how the **b2** pawn has run all the way up the board to win the match in just five moves.

There or roundabouts PAGE 74

The number of ways of reaching each junction is shown in the illustration. Where two or more routes meet, the number of routes is simply added together. So there are ten routes from A to B.

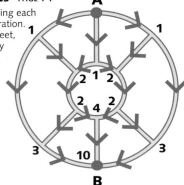

Congestion calamity PAGE 74

Again, the easiest way to solve this is to write down the number of ways of reaching each junction. This is made slightly harder by the arrows pointing in different directions. There are 13 routes in all.

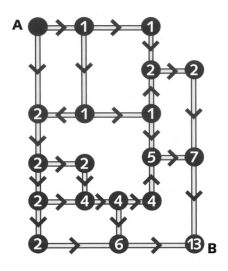

Hungry Horace PAGE 75

In this more difficult puzzle, it was necessary to keep a separate count of the number of routes that have not yet been through a Sloppy Joe's (the upper number in the circles illustrated) as well as the number of routes that have been through exactly one SJ so far (the lower number).

When adding together the number of routes at a junction, the effect of a Sloppy Joe's needs to be taken into account. For example, using the Sloppy Joe's on the far right-hand side, from the west there are two routes that haven't visited SJ yet and three that have. To this we need to add the "3/1" from the north—but note that this turns into a "0/3" when it goes through the SJ (make sure you understand why). This results in [2/3] + [0/3] = [2/6].

By the time we reach the bottom corner, we can see that there are exactly 23 routes that have passed through a Sloppy Joe's exactly once (and six ways of missing one altogether, if you're on a diet).

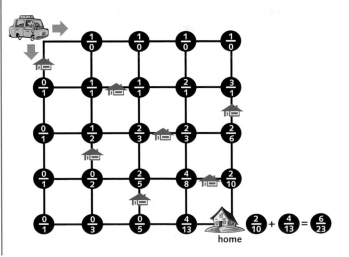

Fare's fair PAGE 76

A It's not difficult to count that there are 10 different routes from A to C, and so there must be 10 from C to B too. As each of these routes is completely independent, there are 10 x 10 = 100 routes from A to B via C.

B Here, we have too many routes to count, but we can use a standard method of writing down the number of ways of reaching a junction, much like the one used for the previous three problems. There is only one way of reaching the north edge of the grid shown and similarly for the east edge. Each intermediate junction is then the sum of the two numbers to the north and east of it.

If we tilt the grid by 45 degrees, we get a pleasant triangular shape in which every number is the sum of the two numbers immediately above it. This is called **Pascal's triangle**, and is useful for all kinds of problems including the lottery result puzzles on page 58. For example, the number of ways of guessing three balls from five possibilities is 10, given by the third number in the fifth row (ignore the top 1).

The illustration shows that there are 210 ways of going from A to B directly. Other interesting by-products of this triangle include the third diagonal (which generates the **triangular numbers**, something else we've seen in this book) and the fourth diagonal (the **pyramid numbers**—i.e., numbers of cannonballs that can be arranged into pyramids with triangular bases).

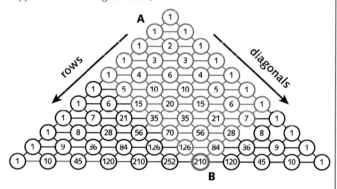

Taxicab geometry PAGE 77

A This is what circles of radii 1, 2, 3, 4, 5, and 6 would look like. Note how "circles" in taxicab geometry look like squares! (Strictly speaking, only the junction points are the circles; the lines between the points are added only to aid the eye.)

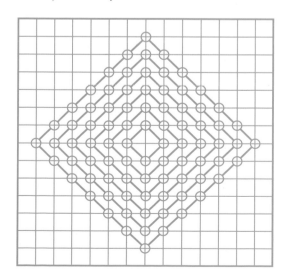

B There are many ways of creating a square in this geometry that all look different. Here are three examples.

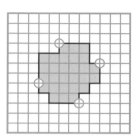

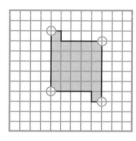
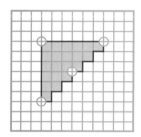

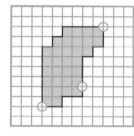

C Here is one example of a 14, 8, 6 triangle in taxicab geometry.

Cake calamity PAGE 80

Because the cake frosting has merely melted and warped but not been mixed in any way, the original and melted designs will be **topologically equivalent**. That is, although they are deformed, the essential design will be the same. So, the number of areas and the ways the lines cross should be familiar.

Cake A: Cake 2 is correct, because in cake 1 the crossroads are in the wrong order and in cake 3 there are too many areas (more than the seven in the original diagram)

Cake B: Cake 2 is correct, because in cake 1 the endpoints don't match and in cake 3 there is a crossroads that shouldn't be there.

Cake C: Cake 2 is correct, because in cake 1 there are six areas (only five in the target diagram) and in cake 3 one line crosses itself, which doesn't happen in the original diagram.

Dough handcuffs PAGE 81

Because we never made or filled in any holes, all these dough models are topologically equivalent to each other.

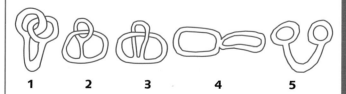

1   2   3   4   5

ANSWERS

Frosting on the cake PAGE 81

These are the frosting designs Cath used. As you can see, each uses three colors.

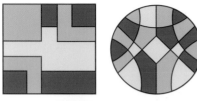

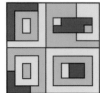

Modern art PAGE 82

A Two colors are required in each case.

B One way to look at this is to add the lines to the painting one by one. As each line is added, all you have to do is to interchange the colors on all regions that lie on **one side** of the new line. This ensures that the colors remain different across old boundaries, and also across the new one thanks to the interchange of colors. The same proof can be generalized to apply to paintings in which the boundaries are either single curves that run right across the whole picture, or closed loops.

Another way of looking at it is to notice that these paintings have an **even** number of edges meeting at any junction. This must be true of any picture that can be colored with just two colors, because the regions around a junction or corner must be of alternate colors. Therefore, any picture can be colored using only two colors if, and only if, all its junctions have an even number of edges meeting there. This is known as the **Two-Color Theorem**.

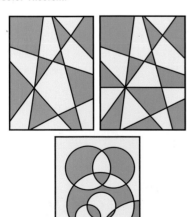

Winning Brams' game PAGE 83

This map is a 2-D equivalent of a dodecahedron (a 12-sided regular solid). The maximizer can always win by playing the same color on the face of the dodecahedron opposite where the opponent last played. The diagram below should make this symmetry clearer.

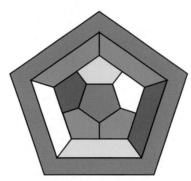

World domination—Part 1

PAGE 84

Here's one way for Sir Frederick's master plan to work:

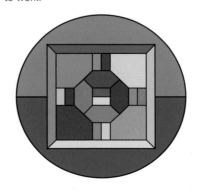

World domination—Part 2

PAGE 84

This is Lord Bertram's view of the world:

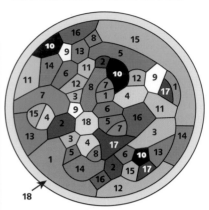

Galactic domination PAGE 85

Nine colors are necessary. 1 & 3 and 2 & 5 are the same colors. Incidentally, this problem was originally proposed by mathematician Gerhard Ringel in 1950.

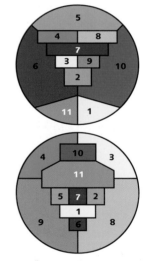

Door to door PAGE 87

Theseus should follow a route such as this:

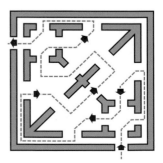

Pythagorean puzzle PAGE 21

Galaxy game PAGE 23

The game of trees   PAGE 28

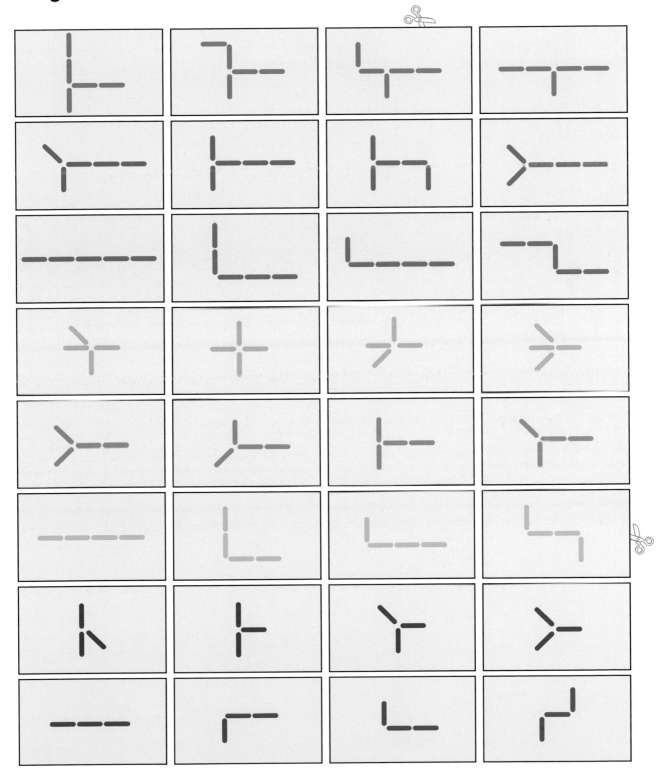

CUTOUTS

The game of trees PAGE 28

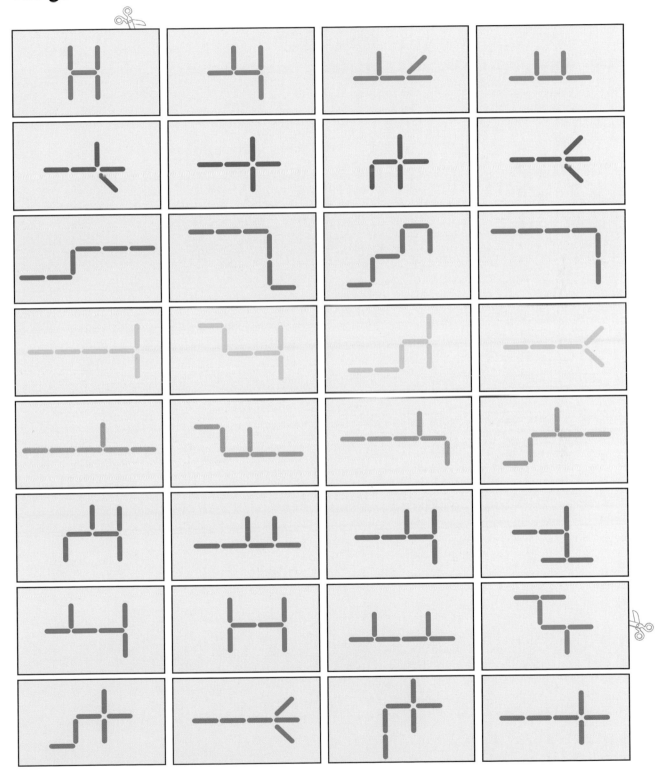

CUTOUTS

Ramsey game board PAGE 31

CUTOUTS

Tangram pieces PAGES 32 AND 34

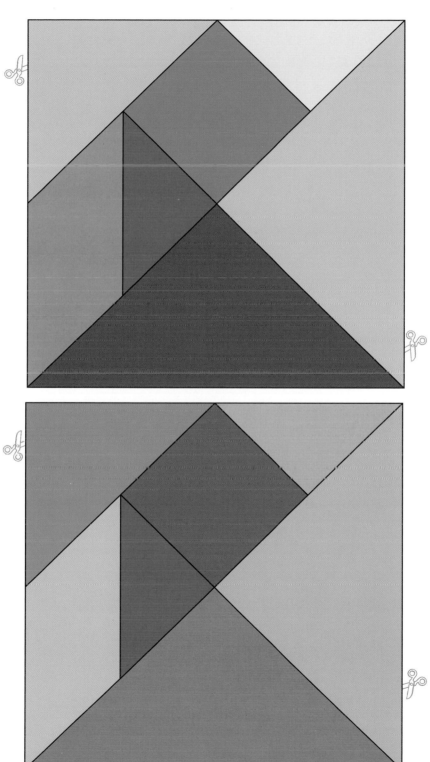

CUTOUTS

Square dissections PAGE 36

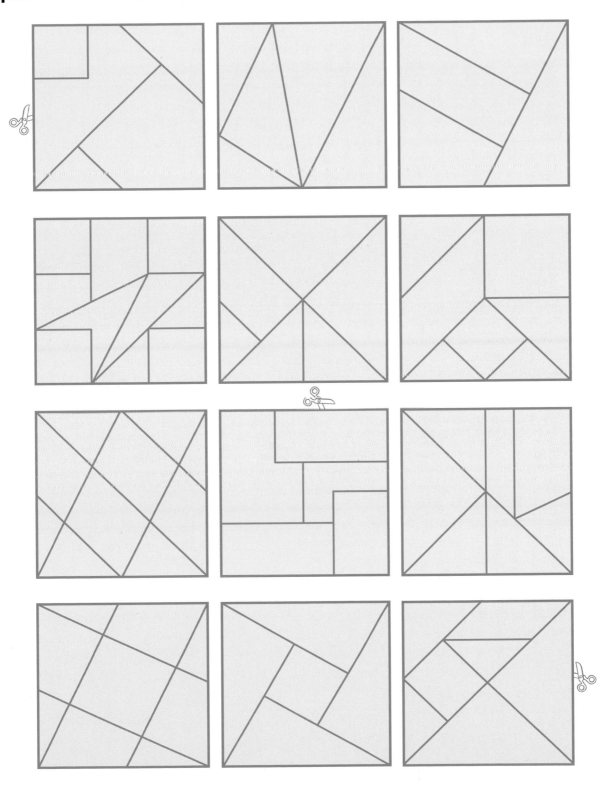

CUTOUTS

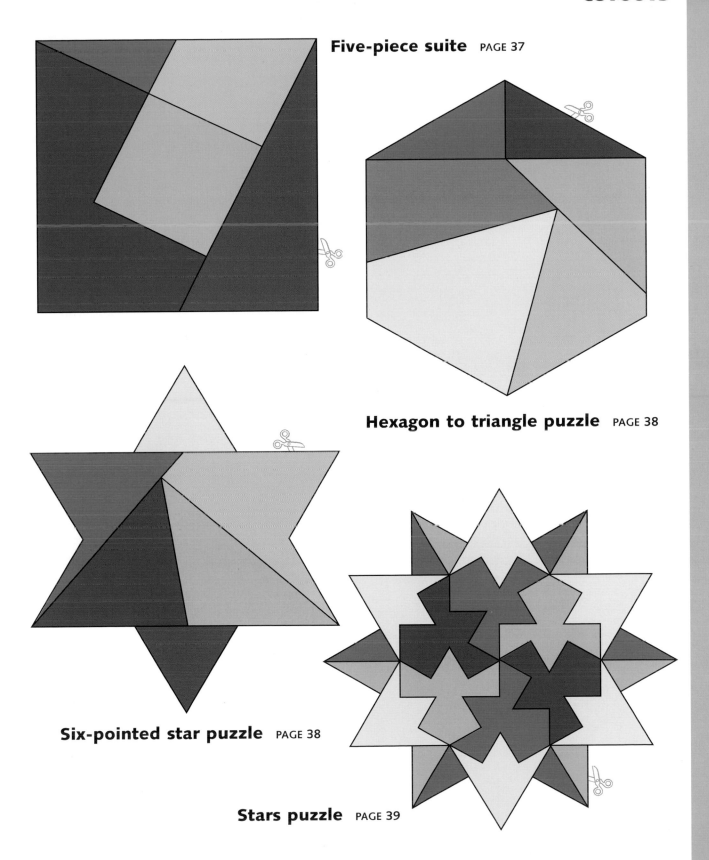

Five-piece suite PAGE 37

Hexagon to triangle puzzle PAGE 38

Six-pointed star puzzle PAGE 38

Stars puzzle PAGE 39

CUTOUTS

Polygo PAGE 46

CUTOUTS

Bits tiles and gameboard PAGES 48–49

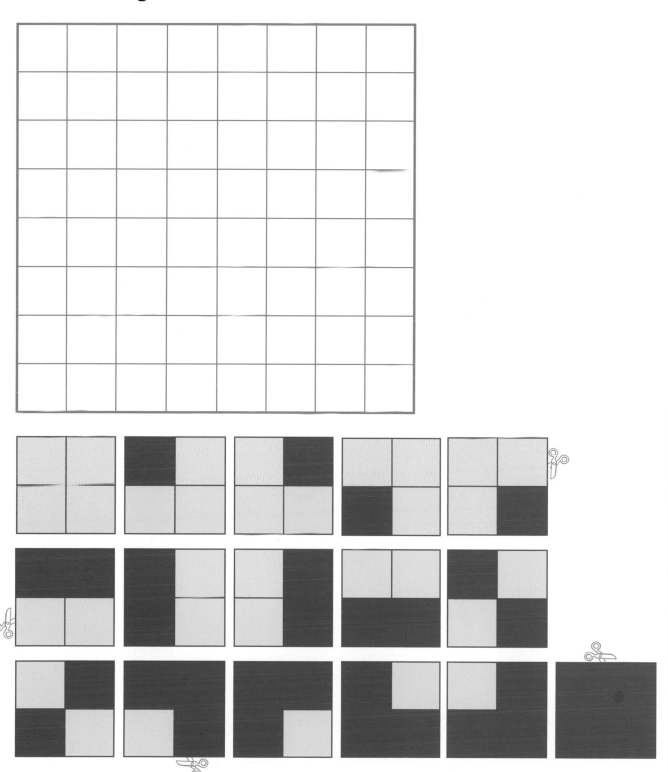

CUTOUTS

Hexabits PAGE 50

CUTOUTS

Domino derby PAGE 52

Domino rally PAGE 53

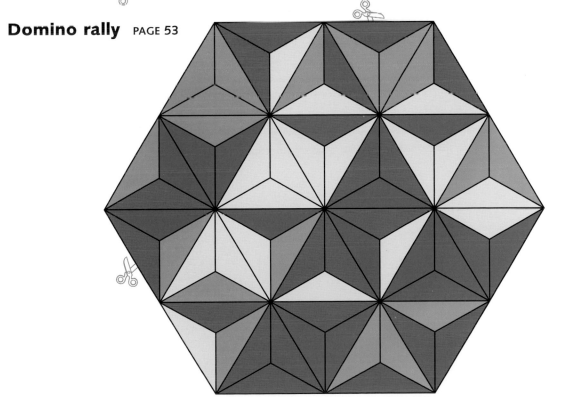

CUTOUTS

Permutino PAGE 58

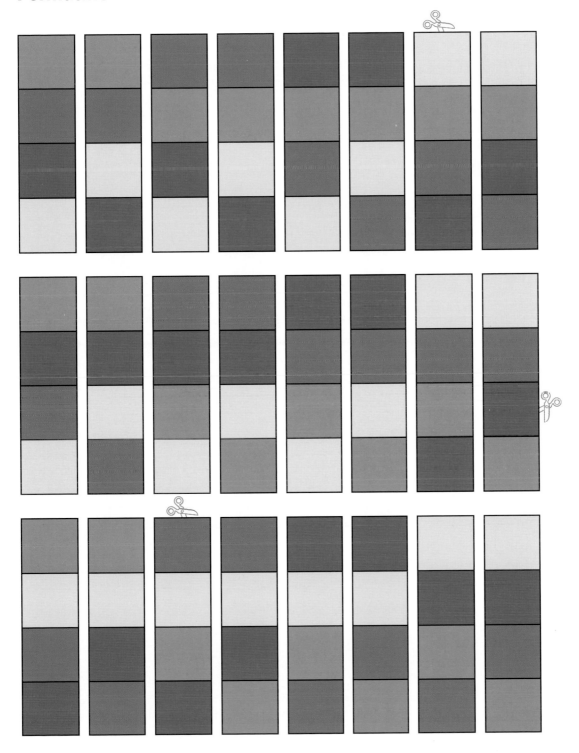

CUTOUTS

Window tiles PAGES 60–61

CUTOUTS

Hexagon tiles PAGES 62–63

CUTOUTS

Dance floor dominoes PAGE 64

DJ display PAGE 65

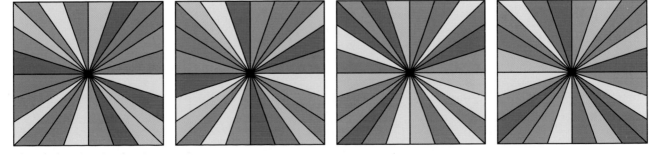